His Spirit Is With Us

I am grateful to all who over the years have taught me, by their insight and example, something about the power and reality of God the Holy Spirit.

I am also grateful to Sue Doggett of the Bible Reading Fellowship for her help and advice and to Debbie Witchell for her patience in typing the manuscript.

HIS SPIRIT IS WITH US

CHRIS NEAL

The Bible Reading Fellowship

Published by
The Bible Reading Fellowship
Peter's Way, Sandy Lane West
Oxford OX4 5HG
ISBN 0 7459 3077 8
Albatross Books Pty Ltd
PO Box 320, Sutherland
NSW 2232, Australia
ISBN 0 7324 0928 4

First edition 1995
10 9 8 7 6 5 4 3 2 1 0

Acknowledgments
Unless otherwise stated, scripture is taken from The Good News Bible published by The Bible Societies/ HarperCollins Publishers Ltd, UK © American Bible Society 1966, 1971, 1976, 1992.

The Holy Bible, New International Version (NIV) copyright © 1973, 1978, 1984 by International Bible Society. Used by permission.

A catalogue record for this book is available from the British Library

Printed and bound in Great Britain by Cox and Wyman Ltd, Reading

CONTENTS

FOREWORD

The Holy Spirit is the great talking point in the Church today, and there are many books relating people's experiences and describing phenomena associated with his work.

This book takes a very different approach. It is concerned with what the *Bible* teaches about the Holy Spirit.

In a thoughtful, but accessible, way it takes the reader through the remarkable story of the impact of the Spirit of God on human beings, human history and the Christian Church. It is a book that needed to be written.

David Winter

People who talk about the presence of the Holy Spirit both attract and threaten many of us. We sense they have a 'secret Christian power' which we would all really like; at the same time we begin to feel insecure—they probably feel we are lacking something.

Chris Neal counteracts this problem with thorough biblical study that roots the individual experience of the Holy Spirit in the person of Jesus and in the community life of the Church. Many readers will find they have enjoyed a real experience of God's Spirit for many years without knowing it as such.

By starting from the anchor point of the Bible, Chris enables the reader to develop a profound and integrated understanding of the Holy Spirit. This is theology without tears.

Chris Sugden
Principal, The Oxford Centre for Mission Studies

INTRODUCTION

The Anglican ASB Communion Service reminds us three times that 'His Spirit is with us'. Whether or not we worship in an Anglican church it is certainly true that God's Holy Spirit is with Christians and that he longs to fill them more and more with his power.

It is equally true that many people are still either confused or even frightened by the Holy Spirit. The aim of this book is to look at the person and work of God the Holy Spirit, to see him clearly in the context of what the Bible teaches about him, and to discover the ways he wants to work in our lives and in the Church today.

Waiting and praying

For the disciples, the period between the ascension and Pentecost was a time of waiting upon God in prayer. They were looking forward to the coming of the Holy Spirit although they had no idea what that entailed.

This study could be used for the six-week period between Ascension and Pentecost, although it can of course be used at any time of the year. God is not limited by the Church's calendar! There is a topic for each week which is divided into seven daily studies. Each day looks at a particular aspect of the Holy Spirit.

The key verses are printed in full at the head of each day's study, but it is recommended that the reader looks up the full Bible passage indicated. Further insight can be gained from the Bible readings listed at the end of each study.

As individuals and as a Church

This is not intended to be simply a book of theory. Each day ends with questions for meditation and prayer. I hope these will help readers to come before the living God and to seek his purpose and will for their lives. When the Holy Spirit came on the day of Pentecost, lives were transformed. The prayer behind this book is that as it is used many will come to experience the power of God the Holy Spirit either for the first time or afresh and that Christian lives and discipleship will be transformed.

This book is designed to be used by churches and house groups as well as by individuals. As Christians we are not called to live in isolation, but to apply our discipleship within the life of the Church. At the end of each week there is material for group discussion and prayer.

Keeping a record

You might like to keep a diary as you follow the course. This will give you the opportunity to jot down particular insights, thoughts and reactions and record growth in your discipleship.

Living the life

In writing this book I have set out to show how the Holy Spirit is rooted in the whole of the Bible and relevant for each one of us today. However he comes to us, it is my prayer that everyone who reads this book will be caught up in the adventure of life lived for God, for indeed, his Spirit is with us.

WEEK 1

THE HOLY SPIRIT IN THE OLD TESTAMENT

For many people the ministry of God the Holy Spirit began at Pentecost, when his power was first seen in all its fulness. From then on the effects of that power became evident in the lives of the apostles and early Christians. Frightened men and women were suddenly transformed. From hiding behind locked doors 'for fear of the Jews', they found themselves propelled into the market place to preach the good news of Jesus and to proclaim boldly the message of salvation.

The day of Pentecost was a significant moment in the work of God, in his world and in the individual. As we will see, the Acts of the Apostles is about the acts of the Holy Spirit in and through the lives of the believers, rather than the acts of individual apostles. However, significant though that day was, it did not stand in isolation but was part of God's ongoing plan for his creation.

In Acts 2, Luke records Peter's first sermon in some detail. In recalling the many allusions to the Old Testament he demonstrated that Jesus was the fulfilment of all the longings and promises of the Old Testament. For us to have any understanding of the person and work of God the Holy Spirit, we must return to the pages of the Old Testament and seek his origins there. It is only in the Old Testament that we can find the keys to unlock many of the secrets of the New.

A closed book

For many Christians the book (or, rather, the books) of the Old Testament remain uncharted territory. We often assume that the Old Testament is difficult to grasp, simply because its contents are so wide and diverse—from love poems to historical documents. Equally, we frequently feel that there is a great distinction between the God of the Old Testament and our understanding of God in the New.

Nevertheless, the Old Testament remains the fundamental foundation upon which the New Testament is built. The Old Testament not only rewards study, it demands it; for unless we understand the great themes it introduces, our grasp of the Christian faith will be shallow and ineffectual. A right approach to the Old Testament is important for our understanding of every aspect of New Testament teaching and doctrine; it is amongst its great themes that the first insights into the work of the Holy Spirit can be found.

One play, two acts

In God's revelation of himself there is continuity between the two Testaments. In no way does the Old close with a sense of failure with the Lord beginning a totally new work with the opening of the New Testament. We will discover that the Old Testament ends with a sense of longing and looking to the future. The New Testament fulfils that longing and shows that the two parts of the Bible are in fact two parts of a whole. Neither can stand in isolation from the other.

As the great themes of the Old Testament were unveiled they prepared the way for the coming of Jesus. He is the great climax of God's work, the focal point of God's revelation and the means of salvation; for the individual and, ultimately, for the whole of creation.

This emphasis on Jesus is the precise nature of the work of the Holy Spirit. He is given not to speak about himself but to point to Jesus—to make Jesus known. There can be no division between the person of Jesus and the person of the Holy Spirit. The Old Testament highlights the aspects of God's work which are empowered by God the Holy Spirit, but ultimately find their focal point in Jesus.

In both Hebrew and Greek the word for 'Spirit' has interchangeable meanings of 'wind', 'breath' and 'spirit'. Within the Old Testament these interchangeable meanings emphasize the fundamental truth about the Spirit of God. He is the wind of God who cannot be controlled or channelled by human beings. It is by God's initiative that he breaks into human situations to achieve God's sovereign will. Whilst it is in the New Testament that the full nature of the Spirit is revealed, throughout the history of the Old Testament his power is evident, not only in the impact he makes on the lives of individuals but also on nations—particularly on the nation of Israel. It is in the pages of the Old Testament that we first encounter the power of the Holy Spirit.

Promise and fulfilment

Promise and fulfilment are two of the themes that will run throughout this week's studies. The Old Testament is a library of promises. Whatever the subject touched on there will always be a pointer to the future and the promise of a more complete revelation and experience of God. This is true of God's Spirit; his power is experienced, his promptings known.

The Holy Spirit is the prime mover behind the great insights of the Old Testament. Each finds its fulfilment in the New Testament in Jesus, all made possible by the power of the Holy Spirit.

Day 1

The Holy Spirit and creation

Genesis 1:1–3

In the beginning, when God created the universe, the earth was formless and desolate. The raging ocean that covered everything was engulfed in total darkness, and the Spirit of God was moving over the water. Then God commanded, 'Let there be light'—and light appeared. (vv. 1–3)

The Old Testament begins with the moment of creation and tells how God created and continues to be involved within his creation. It is at the moment of creation that the work of the Holy Spirit is first seen; it is at this point that our journey of discovery must start. The work of the Holy Spirit has his origins deep in the heart and purposes of God.

The wind of creation

The very first verses of the book of Genesis speak about the Spirit's work and give the first hints of how God is going to reveal himself through the course of history. At the beginning God was present, before the creation of time or space or any of the material world we now experience. The moment of creation was when his breath, or Spirit, began to blow over the chaos to bring order. From the beginning the very nature or personality of God was involved in his creation and his Spirit blew like a mighty hurricane.

The writer in Genesis finds the high point of creation with the coming of human beings. Within the created order humankind was called to have a special relationship with the Creator. This special relationship is to be the gift of God to men and women in every generation. It is as the breath of God is breathed into each one of us that life is given and a relationship of love becomes possible.

A relationship broken and a creation spoilt

As God surveyed his creation he saw that it was perfect and good. But it was into this perfection that sin entered and immediately began to spoil and destroy God's creation. In the account of the Fall, having eaten the fruit Adam and Eve come under God's condemnation, but the result of their disobedience has far wider implications than just for them as individuals.

The images of thorns and thistles and the cursing of the ground are not just childish pictures. The writer saw that the consequences of sin were that the whole of creation had slipped out of focus. No longer were the original harmony and beauty present, for creation had suddenly taken on a darker side.

This brokenness at the heart of creation is a recurring theme throughout the Old Testament. On one hand the writers recognized that the beauty of creation spoke powerfully of the sovereignty and majesty of God: 'How clearly the sky reveals God's glory! How plainly it shows what he has done!' (Psalm 19:1). On the other they recognized that creation could be terrifying, and at the heart of human existence and experience there is pain and suffering. 'Save me, O God! . . . I am sinking in deep mud, and there is no solid ground; I am out in deep water, and the waves are about to drown me' (Psalm 69:1–2).

Reality and renewal

The Bible is totally realistic about the state of the world and human nature. It never shirks from telling it as it is—whether that is to do with the weakness of an individual, or the disobedience of a nation, or the violence which stalks creation. However, alongside this realism there is a constant longing for renewal and for the whole of creation to be restored.

In the book of Isaiah this longing finds its focal point in the coming of the Lord's servant, who would restore the social order with justice and fairness and renew creation. Even more significantly, Isaiah foretold that the Lord's servant would be anointed by the Lord's Spirit.

The longing and fulfilment—a new creation

The promise of the Spirit-filled servant who would renew the whole of creation found its fulfilment of course in Jesus, who came as the Word made flesh, anointed by the power of the Holy Spirit: 'Through the Son then God decided to bring the whole universe back to himself. God made peace through his Son's blood on the cross and so brought back to himself all things, both on earth and in heaven' (Colossians 1:20).

The cross will have its final victory when Christ returns and makes all things new. In the meantime, as we await this final triumph, it is the Holy Spirit, present at the moment of creation, who enables us to long and yearn for the restoration of that creation.

Further reading

Genesis 2:7; Job 26:13; Psalm 104:30; Colossians 1:17

Pause for thought

Take time to be still and reflect on the readings and the study. The suggestion to keep a diary or note book will give you the opportunity to record the most important things that have struck you. It will also help you keep a record of how you might want to respond to God's Holy Spirit.

Pause for reflection

Take time to reflect on the beauty and power of creation and how creation itself speaks of the Creator. List the many ways in which creation is broken and pray for all who are caught up in the suffering of this present age. Remember that through his anointed servant, the Lord will restore the whole of creation.

Pause for prayer

Lord God,
thank you that your creating Spirit
brought order out of chaos.
Thank you that your creating Spirit
continues to bring light in darkness
and hope in suffering.
Thank you that through your anointed servant
you will restore all things.
In Jesus' name
Amen.

Day 2

The Holy Spirit and the covenant

Jeremiah 31:31–34

The Lord says, 'The time is coming when I will make a new covenant with the people of Israel and with the people of Judah. It will not be like the old covenant that I made with their ancestors when I took them by the hand and led them out of Egypt. Although I was like a husband to them, they did not keep that covenant. The new covenant that I will make with the people of Israel will be this: I will put my law within them and write it on their hearts.' **(vv. 31–33)**

An understanding of covenant is one of those important foundation stones which must be laid if we are really to understand God's purposes in the Old and New Testaments, and indeed our own discipleship.

What is a covenant?

The word 'covenant' simply means an agreement between two people. Today it has overtones of financial promises and legal agreements, but in the Old Testament it meant an understanding or relationship which was binding on both parties. The idea of covenant was not limited to Israel, but there are distinctive features in the way Israel understood the covenant with the Lord God.

In other nations covenants were usually between parties of equal status. Both sides brought demands and a compromise was reached by negotiation. In the Old Testament the covenant is made between God and individuals or with the nation itself, but at no time is the covenant seen as an agreement between equals. The history of the Old Testament is the story of the development of the covenant which eventually found its completion in Jesus.

The hitch-hikers guide to the covenant

In the space of a few short sentences we need to cover thousands of years of history, so of necessity detail will be limited! However, it is important to see the highlights as the history of the Old Testament unfolds.

A covenant with Noah. In the story of Noah we see the first covenant which God made with a person. Before the flood, the covenant spoke of God's promise to preserve Noah and his family, and, after the flood, the covenant spoke of God's promise never again to destroy his creation. It is important to recognize that this covenant, as with its future developments, was entirely the work of God's grace and initiative; human beings could make no contribution except by their obedience.

A covenant with Abraham. Again, the covenant is God's initiative and is with one person. On this occasion however, there is the promise to Abraham's descendants and the fact that they will need to be saved from a foreign land. Salvation becomes closely linked with the covenant.

A covenant with Moses. With the coming of Moses there is a great act of salvation as the people are led from slavery in Egypt. Later the giving of the Law becomes linked with the covenant. Some have seen this as a radical departure from the previous covenants because it seems to suggest that the agreement is no longer reliant on God's grace but on the keeping of the Law. (This was to become the emphasis of Pharisaic teaching.) The point is that a holy God demands that the people related to him need to reflect his holiness and righteousness. Obedience to the Law does not ratify the covenant, rather entering into the covenant should encourage people to live a holy life.

The covenant with David. The covenant's expectation of holy living proved too great a demand for God's people. Even the great King David, who ushered in a period of prosperity for Israel and who had an especially close relationship with God, demonstrated the inability of men and women to live a holy life. This great leader proved that he too was a weak and fallible human being. Following his adulterous affair with Bathsheba and his willingness to murder her husband, he recognized that a greater and holier king was required.

With David comes the longing for a true king who would establish the covenant with God in holiness and righteousness.

What's wrong with the covenant?

The simple answer is 'nothing'! What was wrong was the frailty of human beings and their inability to live the holy life required by the holy God.

As the Old Testament drew to a close the messianic hope of King David was beginning to be sounded by the prophets. Jeremiah and Ezekiel recognized that the people had failed to keep the covenant and that God's great 'manifesto', the Law, simply highlighted the weakness of human nature. They taught that there was a need for a new covenant, a covenant written deep in the hearts and lives of men and women and no longer on tablets of stone.

The only way in which the covenant can be 'written' on the hearts of people is by the ministry of the Holy Spirit. The Holy Spirit alone can warm the heart and direct us into the ways of heaven.

The longing and fulfilment—a new covenant

Jesus was the one who would fulfil the messianic dreams of King David and bring in a new kingdom in the power of his Holy Spirit, as the anointed one of the Lord. By his death Jesus alone could bring about the new covenant. In the upper room as he gathered with his disciples for the Last Supper, he said, 'This cup is God's new covenant sealed with my blood, which is poured out for you' (Luke 22:20).

At this point history takes on a real significance for the present moment and our own discipleship. As disciples, as part of the Lord's people, we need to enter this new covenant on a daily basis. We are all aware of our own weakness and frailty and, with Paul, we have to say: 'I don't do the good I want to do; instead, I do the evil that I do not want to do' (Romans 7:19).

It is at this point of brokenness that we need to open ourselves to the ministry and power of the Holy Spirit and allow him to write the new covenant upon our hearts.

Further reading
Genesis 9:1–17; 15:1–6; Jeremiah 42:1–12; Ezekiel 36:24–38

Pause for thought
Through Jesus, and by the power of the Holy Spirit, God has made a new covenant possible, the way is open for you to enjoy a new and special relationship with God. Write down your response in your diary.

Pause for reflection
Jesus is the continuing covenant between God and human beings. The Holy Spirit wants to write that special relationship deep within our lives. How do you want to respond?

Pause for prayer
God of Noah, Abraham, Moses and David,
thank you that you never give up
in your love for your creation.
Thank you that you fulfilled your purposes
in the Lord Jesus Christ.
Thank you that your Holy Spirit
makes the new covenant possible.
Come today and write your words
deep in my heart and life.
For Jesus' sake
Amen.

Day 3

The Holy Spirit and the people of God

Isaiah 58:1–7

'The kind of fasting I want is this: remove the chains of oppression and the yoke of injustice, and let the oppressed go free. Share your food with the hungry and open your homes to the homeless poor. Give clothes to those who have nothing to wear, and do not refuse to help your own relatives.' (vv. 6–7)

Yesterday's gallop through the history of Israel, tracing the development of the covenant, showed that God wanted a relationship with his own people. Today the spotlight is turned on that relationship as we explore something of its meaning. God wanted to enter into a special relationship—a covenant relationship—for a purpose.

A special people for a special purpose

From the very beginning of history it is clear that God wanted a special relationship with his creation. The writer in Genesis sees the high point of creation as the making of Adam and Eve in God's own image. 'In the image of God' means that we have a spiritual dimension to our lives, enabling us to relate to our Creator in a particular way. We are also created with the ability to make decisions about right and wrong.

The Fall brought that special relationship with God to an end. But, even after this disastrous event, God longed to restore the relationship. In the cool of the evening he calls 'Adam, where are you?' Those words have been echoing down the centuries and are still sounding today.

Although judgment and punishment followed this disobedience, the rest of the Old and New Testament is the account of God's longing and working to re-establish his friendship with sinful men and women.

Yesterday saw how God worked with Noah, Abraham, Moses and David to create a covenant not just with them as individuals but, through them, with the whole nation. It was God's desire that he should have a people who were especially chosen by him to be his own. All the verses suggested for today emphasize this calling. Deuteronomy 14:2 simply underlines the truth; God called Israel to be a special people under his authority: 'For you are a people holy to the Lord your God. Out of all the peoples on the face of the earth, the Lord has chosen you to be his treasured possession' (NIV).

Throughout the Old Testament there is always an awareness of that special relationship. Although the people frequently wandered from that calling there were always those who would call them back to their true vocation. However, it would appear that very few understood the purpose of their calling. We find the clue to its purpose in the book of Isaiah: 'Nations will come to your light, and kings to the brightness of your dawn' (Isaiah 60:3, NIV).

The prophet looked forward to a glorious future, but he recognized that the people of Israel had failed to be what God wanted them to be. The calling was not to make them exclusive and arrogant but rather to encourage them in humility to shine in the light of God's glory so that others could see his truth.

Privilege and responsibility

Many of the Old Testament prophets made it clear that whilst the people might be standing upon the privilege of the special status with God, they were consistently failing to fulfil the responsibilities laid upon them. In the passage at the beginning of today's study the prophet says that the people kept to the outer forms of their faith and indeed maintained all the religious observances, but they failed to recognize the implications of their relationship with the living God. They were maintaining the fasts but failing to feed the hungry and provide for the poor.

The longing and fulfilment—the true people of God

Before we shake our finger too vigorously at the people of Israel we should remember that they failed to live out their calling as God's people because of inherent human weakness. In the Old Testament the power of the Holy Spirit is usually only given to individuals in particular circumstances. There is no sense in which all the people have the empowering of the Holy Spirit so that their inherent weakness can be transformed into glorious obedience to God's will and calling.

On several occasions within the Old Testament the longing is expressed that the Holy Spirit might be given to the many. By the time of Joel—a prophet who lived at the end of the Old Testament history—there was a longing and expectation that God's Spirit would be poured out on everyone so they could truly become God's people: 'And afterwards, I will pour out my Spirit on all people. Your sons and daughters will prophesy, your old men will dream dreams, your young men will see visions. Even on my servants, both men and women, I will pour out my Spirit in those days' (Joel 2:28–29, NIV).

On the day of Pentecost, Peter took up Joel's prophesy, declaring that God had kept his promise and that the Holy Spirit had come in all his fulness. As the Spirit fell, so he empowered those who received him to become the new community of God's people, both Jew and Gentile; a community which celebrated the privileges and, almost without realizing it, worked out the responsibilities.

This is our contact point for today. All Christians are called to be the people of God and to shine his glory and light into a dark world and to proclaim his good news. This calling to be his people echoes from the beginning of creation and can only be fulfilled if we are prepared to open ourselves to the gift of the Holy Spirit foretold by Joel.

Further reading

Genesis 12:1–3; Exodus 19:5–6; Deuteronomy 14:2; Isaiah 42:6; 60:3

Pause for thought

Think about what it means to be part of God's new community. Are you prepared to work out the responsibilities as well as knowing more of the privileges? Be honest and write your response in your diary.

Pause for reflection

God's Holy Spirit longs to make us pure and holy so that God's light can be seen by all people. What prevents you from living in this way?

Pause for prayer

Lord, the light of your love is shining,
In the midst of the darkness, shining;

Lord, may your people be so filled with your Holy Spirit
that every dark place may see your light.
Amen.

Day 4

The Holy Spirit and kingship

Isaiah 11:1–9

The royal line of David is like a tree that has been cut down; but just as new branches sprout from a stump, so a new king will arise from among David's descendants. The spirit of the Lord will give him wisdom, and the knowledge and skill to rule his people. He will know the Lord's will and honour him, and find pleasure in obeying him. **(vv. 1–3)**

To understand the Old Testament we need to review it in great sweeps of history. This has been the case with the study of the covenant and the development of Israel as the people of God. It will also be the case as we turn to look at the idea of kingship.

The two previous themes have found their focal point in Jesus and the work of the Holy Spirit. In today's study we will discover that the same is true for kingship.

God's leaders for God's people

In the early part of Israel's history, leadership was seen to be God's, although this was often mediated through particular individuals. For example, in the Exodus, God took the initiative and gave the guidance, but it was his servant Moses who explained God's purposes to the people and brought the needs of the people to the Lord.

After crossing the Jordan and entering into the Promised Land the same pattern continued with the leadership of Joshua and then the judges. The Old Testament shows us that leadership was divinely appointed and divinely empowered. The book of Numbers tells how Moses knew the Spirit of the Lord and how that Spirit was eventually shared with those called to help him. Similarly Joshua, Moses' successor, was filled with God's Spirit, as were the judges Gideon, Jephtha and Samson. The last great judge was the prophet Samuel and it was during his time that the people asked for a king.

Give us a king!

The request for a king saddened Samuel who saw it as a rejection of the Lord's leadership. However the request was granted and so began the long saga of the kings of Israel and Judah with their chequered history of strength and weakness, success and failure, often linked to their willingness or otherwise to obey the Lord.

In all the history of kingship two important things stand out. First, the kings were always called to be under the Lord's authority. Not all obeyed that injunction but some recognized that they held authority simply because of the authority of the Lord. In many ways they were seen as regents rather than kings in their own right.

Secondly, the anointing of kings with oil was often accompanied by an outpouring of the Spirit of God. When Saul was anointed he found himself with a group of prophets, prophesying in the power of the Holy Spirit (1 Samuel 10). Similarly the Holy Spirit came upon David and continued to empower him at various points in his life. Although there is no direct record of the Holy Spirit filling Solomon, the Lord filled him with wisdom—frequently linked with the Spirit of God.

The once and future king

The history of Israel's kings is a sorry tale of disobedience and apostasy. So it is that by the end of the Old Testament the authority of a king over Israel had disappeared and the Jewish nation found itself under the rule of various surrounding states and empires.

As this sorry state of affairs developed there was a longing within Israel for the true king to come. People looked back to the glorious time of King David and looked forward for one who would come from his line to rule as David had done. Over the years this longed-for king became linked with the Messiah, God's anointed one. The people looked for the new kingdom and reign he would usher in.

Like David, the Messiah king would know the power of God's Holy Spirit, but, unlike David and the other kings, this new king would rule with perfection and justice and for ever. A time of peace and justice would be established and his light would be a light for all nations and would bring salvation to all people. The Messiah king would also be a servant who God's Spirit would enable to proclaim the good news to the poor, and freedom to those who were captives.

It was an amazing vision as it developed over the long centuries of Israel's history. It was a vision that was to find its fulfilment in Jesus.

The longing and fulfilment—the true king

In Psalm 110 David declares: 'The Lord says to my Lord: "Sit at my right hand until I make your enemies a footstool for your feet"' (Psalm 110:1, NIV). David recognized the power of the Holy Spirit and longed for the coming of the true king. That longing was fulfilled in Jesus, who clearly identified himself as the longed-for Messiah. When he was challenged by the Pharisees about the descent of the Messiah, Jesus referred to this verse and showed how David saw the Messiah as divinely superior to himself (Matthew 22:41–46).

The resurrection declares that Jesus is indeed Lord of all creation, time and eternity. In him God's kingdom has come. The reign of the true king has begun.

Further reading

1 Samuel 16:1–3; Matthew 22:41–46

Pause for thought

Jesus is God's appointed and Spirit-filled king. Do you recognize his sovereignty and rule in your life? In your diary, note down areas of your life where Jesus is not allowed to reign. Be honest before God and with yourself.

Pause for reflection

Does the Church recognize the kingship of Jesus? What should this mean in its everyday life?

Pause for prayer

Father, your kingdom come on earth as it is in heaven.

Father, we often pray these words.
Teach us to recognize Jesus as your anointed king
and to allow his rule in our hearts, lives
and in the midst of your people, the church. Amen.

Day 5

The Holy Spirit and prophecy

Isaiah 6:1–8

I said, 'There is no hope for me! I am doomed because every word that passes my lips is sinful, and I live among a people whose every word is sinful. And yet, with my own eyes, I have seen the King, the Lord Almighty!' Then one of the creatures flew down to me, carrying a burning coal that he had taken from the altar with a pair of tongs. He touched my lips with the burning coal and said, 'This has touched your lips, and now your guilt is gone, and your sins are forgiven.' Then I heard the Lord say, 'Whom shall I send? Who will be our messenger?' I answered, 'I will go! Send me!' **(vv. 5–8)**

Sometimes in the Old Testament God's power was demonstrated in dramatic and even disturbing ways, but at no time was that power mindless or irrational. The power of the Holy Spirit comes with a purpose and flows from the heart of a personal, loving and gracious God.

A word from the Lord

The Lord's underlying desire is to make himself known and live in communion with us. The Holy Spirit moves in the world so that the Creator might communicate with the created. Throughout history God has been speaking to his world. It is in the coming together of his word and his Spirit that his true nature can be seen. At the very moment of creation we can see the word of God and the Spirit of God working together, each enriching the other.

It is not only at the moment of creation that word and Spirit are held together. Throughout the Old Testament, the true prophet was consumed by the word of the Lord and was able to speak boldly because of the power of the Holy Spirit. Hence David in a moment of prophetic anointing could say: 'The Spirit of the Lord speaks through me; his message is on my lips' (2 Samuel 23:2).

Under conviction

Whilst not all of the prophets speak explicitly of the Holy Spirit empowering their ministry, all of them experience this divine compulsion and are impelled to speak out no matter what the cost.

Jeremiah was called to be a prophet as a young man. During the moment of his call he imagined all the excuses he might make and heard the Lord answering them one by one. He was called to the ministry of prophecy knowing he would be reviled and persecuted, and yet would remain faithful for the many years of his life. His conviction and faithfulness stemmed from the simple fact that he knew the word of the Lord deep in his heart and life: 'The Lord stretched out his hand, touched my lips, and said to me, "Listen, I am giving you the words you must speak"' (Jeremiah 1:9).

Similarly, Ezekiel heard and knew the word of the Lord and also experienced the power of the Holy Spirit resting on him. His prophecy opens with the words: 'I heard the Lord speak to me and I felt his power' (Ezekiel 1:3). The whole of the book of Ezekiel is the Lord speaking through dramatic visions by the power of the Holy Spirit; speaking his word to the heart of the prophet.

The book of Isaiah shows the same pattern. Seemingly unexpectedly, the prophet received a vision of the Lord. In that vision he recognized the holiness of God and his own unworthiness. However, repentance was followed by cleansing not just by the word of God, but also by the fire of God. This new beginning was followed immediately by the prophet's willingness to become a messenger for God. His meeting with the living God had left him no choice. He felt compelled to proclaim the Lord's word by the power of his Spirit. Towards the end of the book of Isaiah, the prophet declared: '"Now come close to me and hear what I say. From the beginning I have spoken openly, and have always made my words come true." (Now the Sovereign Lord has given me his power and sent me)' (Isaiah 48:16).

A clearer picture

In the Old Testament the prophet was not there to be a superior fortune-teller. The work of the prophet was to make God's will known—usually in a particular circumstance or to a particular individual. The prophet was there to warn, reprimand, encourage or give hope. Underlying the immediate purpose, prophecy built up over the centuries to give a fuller and clearer picture of the character and purposes of God. The sum of the prophetic ministry was that God *was* revealed and made known.

In this way the Old Testament prophets were preparing the way for the time when God's revelation of himself would be completed fully in Jesus.

The longing and fulfilment—the Word made flesh

The writer to the Hebrews says that in the Old Testament God spoke in varied and fragmentary ways over many centuries. The exciting truth is that all this preparatory work comes to fruition with the birth of Jesus. The remarkable thing about Jesus is not that he was another prophet speaking God's word, but rather he was the actual embodiment of God's Word in human flesh and as such he radiated and reflected God's glory. So John could declare: 'The Word became a human being and, full of grace and truth, lived among us. We saw his glory, the glory which he received as the Father's only Son' (John 1:14).

In Jesus the full Word of God was revealed. The longings of the centuries were over. The Word made flesh was anointed and empowered by God's Holy Spirit; truly Word and Spirit came together: 'The one whom God has sent speaks God's words, because God gives him the fullness of his Spirit' (John 3:34).

Further reading

Micah 3:8

Pause for thought

Jesus is God's living Word. Are you prepared to listen to him? Write down your feelings and response in your diary.

Pause for reflection

God is a God who speaks a living Word. Jesus, God's living Word, reflected the fulness of the Holy Spirit in his life and work. What are the implications of these truths for your discipleship today?

Pause for prayer

Lord, help me today
to be willing to listen
to the promptings of your Holy Spirit,
that I might hear your word.
Lord, when I hear your word
help me to obey willingly.
Amen.

Day 6

The Holy Spirit and the presence of God

Ezekiel 47:1–12

The man led me back to the entrance of the Temple. Water was coming out from under the entrance and flowing east, the direction the Temple faced... He said to me, 'This water flows through the land to the east and down into the Jordan Valley and to the Dead Sea. When if flows into the Dead Sea, it replaces the salt water of that sea with fresh water. Wherever the stream flows, there will be all kinds of animals and fish. The stream will make the water of the Dead Sea fresh, and wherever it flows, it will bring life.' **(vv. 1, 8–9)**

From the earliest history of Israel there is the expectation that God will be present with his people. Various symbols are used to express this. For example, the altar that Abraham built at Mamre, and the stone that Jacob set up after his vision at Bethel when he fled from Esau, are both symbols which point to God's presence in a given situation.

God—present with his people

With the ministry of Moses and the Israelites' escape from Egypt, this understanding of the Lord's presence amongst his people became more explicit and formalized. The heart of the nation was considered to be the tabernacle or the tent of the presence. It was here that Moses would speak to the Lord on behalf of the people. It was a constant reminder to the whole nation that not only was God with them but they were dependent upon him for guidance and provision, as they travelled to the Promised Land. This is underlined in Leviticus: 'I will put my dwelling-place among you, and I will not abhor you. I will walk among you and be your God, and you will be my people' (Leviticus 26:11–12, NIV).

With the settlement in the Promised Land, the nomadic, temporary tent of the presence was eventually replaced by the permanent temple in Jerusalem. Solomon, fulfilling the wishes of his father, David, built the temple. Whilst there was recognition that buildings could never contain the God of heaven and earth, there was an expectation that God would dwell in the temple amongst his people.

The Old Testament records Solomon's long prayer at the dedication of the temple and says: 'When Solomon finished praying, fire came down from heaven and consumed the burnt offering and the sacrifices, and the glory of the Lord filled the temple. The priests could not enter the temple of the Lord because the glory of the Lord filled it' (2 Chronicles 7:1–2, NIV).

It was a dramatic moment as the Lord's presence moved into the temple in glory and in the power of the Holy Spirit. When the Holy Spirit moved in such a powerful way the response was that the people fell down and worshipped in recognition of his sovereignty and might. The first temple was not a mere physical building, it was a symbol of God's dwelling amongst the people in all his power.

The glory removed

The history of Israel is, of course, the unhappy catalogue of sinful rebellion and disobedience. The prophets tell of God's displeasure and warn of the coming judgment in the form of exile (first the people from the northern tribes of Israel were taken to Assyria, and then the people from the southern tribe of Judah to Babylon).

The prophet Ezekiel spoke out in the crucial years when Judah was taken into captivity and the first temple fell. In one of his visions, Ezekiel, caught up by the Holy Spirit, saw the glory of the Lord leaving the temple: 'Then the glory of the Lord departed from over the threshold of the temple and stopped above the cherubim. While I watched, the cherubim spread their wings and rose from the ground' (Ezekiel 10:18–19, NIV).

The language is full of imagery and difficult to understand fully, but the truth behind the words is clear. The Lord's glory and power which came to the temple to dwell amongst the nation in the time of Solomon was removed in the days of Ezekiel. The temple was to be destroyed utterly by the Babylonians. The more horrifying truth was that God withdrew his Holy Spirit and glory from amongst his people.

A new vision and a new temple

Although a century later, in the time of Zechariah, the physical temple was rebuilt in Jerusalem, the Jews themselves never believed that the Holy Spirit and the glory of the Lord returned. However, the last part of the book of Ezekiel is concerned with the new temple, the new Jerusalem, and the certainty that the Lord's power would return and that he would once again be present amongst his people. Ezekiel 47 is particularly significant. The prophet saw the river of water flowing from the very heart of the temple and into the surrounding countryside and eventually into the Dead Sea. This river seemed miraculous because it became deeper and more powerful, even though there were no tributaries. It brought life wherever it flowed, even to the lifeless Dead Sea.

Water was seen as a symbol of God's power, but this vision was going to be invested with great significance in Jesus. Again the Old Testament pointed forward to a fulfilment yet to come. The Holy Spirit never returned to the temple in Jerusalem, but Ezekiel proclaimed boldly that there would be a new temple and it would be the source of the power of God as his Spirit moved like a mighty river out into a thirsty land.

The longing and the fulfilment—the new temple

After many seemingly silent years the Lord God acted decisively in the coming of Jesus. Once again he was present amongst his people.

In John 2 there is a discussion between Jesus and the religious leaders, following Jesus' cleansing of the temple. Jesus challenged them to tear down the temple, saying he would rebuild it in three days. Jesus was talking about his body. The glory and the presence of God no longer dwelt in a temple built by hands. God was making himself known in and through Jesus. The new permanent temple had come, and men and women could at last come into the very presence of God as they met with his living Word, Jesus Christ.

Further reading
Exodus 33:7–11; Leviticus 26:11–12; Ezekiel 10:18–19; John 7:38

Pause for thought
In Jesus Christ, God came and dwelt amongst men and women. Do you acknowledge the uniqueness of Jesus? In your diary write down your reactions to this claim.

Pause for reflection
The power of God moves amongst us because of his work in and through Jesus Christ. What are the implications for us today of Jesus' staggering claim that he was the true temple of God?

Pause for prayer
Lord Jesus Christ,
thank you that, as you dwelt amongst us,
you revealed the glory and power of God himself.
Help us to understand this deep mystery.
Amen.

Day 7

The Holy Spirit and hope

Ezekiel 37:1–10

I felt the powerful presence of the Lord, and his spirit took me and set me down in a valley where the ground was covered with bones. He led me all round the valley, and I could see that there were very many bones and that they were very dry. He said to me, 'Mortal man, can these bones come back to life?' I replied, 'Sovereign Lord, only you can answer that!' **(vv. 1–3)**

The book of Ezekiel is not one of unmitigated gloom and doom. Indeed, wherever God's word of judgment is spoken in the Old Testament it is always shot through with the possibility of renewal and restoration if there is true repentance. Ezekiel was sure that God's purposes could not ultimately be thwarted by the disobedience of men and women. He believed that Israel would be restored, despite their disobedience, for the sake of God's glory: 'Therefore say to the house of Israel, "This is what the sovereign Lord says: It is not for your sake, O house of Israel, that I am going to do these things, but for the sake of my holy name" ' (Ezekiel 36:22, NIV).

It is against this background that we turn to chapter 37. The vision came not from his own mind or intellect, but was given to him by the intervention of the Lord working by his Holy Spirit. Ezekiel was asked: 'Can these bones come back to life?' (37:3). In his reply, Ezekiel recognized that only the Lord could do a new thing for broken and shattered Israel. The prophet was given the task of declaring God's word to the lifeless bones. As he did so, the bones began to move and shake; the skeletons were formed and then covered with flesh and muscle. But Ezekiel saw that, whilst the bones had come together, there was still no life.

Ezekiel was then called to speak to the wind. The Holy Spirit moved, the wind blew, and lifeless skeletons became alive like a mighty army. The prophet brought together yet again the word and the Spirit. He proclaimed the word of God and the Spirit moved to bring life to the people of God.

The second part of the chapter speaks of what will be. Ezekiel looked for the day when the divided and scattered people of God would be gathered together under the rule of the messianic king: 'A king like my servant David will be their king. They will all be united under one ruler and will obey my laws faithfully' (Ezekiel 37:24).

The longing and fulfilment—the living hope

In Jesus, the Messiah—the Christ—has come in the power of the Holy Spirit. The fulfilment has begun but has not yet been completed. The full messianic kingdom will be ushered in with the return of Jesus Christ, when every eye will behold him and every tongue will confess his Lordship. The book of Revelation takes up Ezekiel's song and sings his words to tell of the final victory of God as it speaks of the new heaven and the new earth.

Throughout its history the Old Testament witnesses to the character and work of God's Spirit, reflecting every facet of God's revelation of himself, and always pointing forwards to the great fulfilment in the person of Jesus Christ. In Jesus the age of the Spirit has dawned in all its fulness. We must be ready to explore that fulness, to allow the Spirit to touch our lives as he wants, and to allow him to fill us afresh with his hope as we look for the completion of his work.

Pause for thought

Be still, and as you breathe in, imagine you are breathing in the Holy Spirit of God. Reflect on what this means to you. Write down your response in your diary.

Pause for reflection

The power of the Holy Spirit helps us to see God at work in the present moment. Are you willing to allow the Holy Spirit to fill and renew you day by day?

Pause for prayer

Lord, so fill me with your Holy Spirit
that I might know your living hope
both for the present and for all eternity.
Amen.

Material for group study

For sharing

As individuals within the group, note down:

◇ the things that have been new to you and enlightened you

◇ the questions that have been raised.

Divide the group into pairs and give time for each pair to share their answers. Come together as a whole group for discussion and sharing.

For learning

On pieces of card, write down the key words for each of the day's studies—covenant, kingship and so on. Underneath each heading write down ways in which these themes should influence your individual discipleship and your life as a church.

For discussion and application

Divide into pairs again and discuss how the things learnt above should actually be applied to your congregation. What differences does the Holy Spirit want to make?

For prayer

Take each of the topics raised as a subject for prayer. The leader might want to lead in prayer or give opportunities for members to pray. If the group is not used to praying aloud, the pairs could write prayers for each topic.

WEEK 2

THE HOLY SPIRIT IN JESUS

Last week's studies explored the work of the Holy Spirit in the Old Testament and saw how God's power broke into the lives of individuals and nations. Whilst the Holy Spirit remained a shadowy, elusive figure in many ways, there was always the sense that God's power was at work.

The rabbis at the time of Jesus were teaching that with the prophets Haggai, Zechariah and Malachi the voice of God's Spirit had fallen silent and his power had been withdrawn. From the end of the Old Testament until the beginning of the New the people of Israel (or at least a faithful remnant) were looking for the coming of God's kingdom and for the Lord to act in a new and decisive way. It is against this background that we turn to the coming of Jesus and his ministry.

Jesus—the focal point

Before it is possible to understand the significance and purpose of God's Holy Spirit in our own lives, or in the life of the Church, it is important to look at the ministry and the life of Jesus. It is in the life of Jesus that we can discover the vitality of the Holy Spirit and eventually learn principles which can be applied to our discipleship today. Jesus is the giver of God's Holy Spirit and the model and pattern of his work.

Jesus was not born into a vacuum. He is the focal point of God's plan for his creation and is part of his continuing work of revelation and redemption. In their Gospels, both Matthew and Luke give the ancestry of Jesus (Matthew 1; Luke 3). Most of the time we simply skip over these as boring and irrelevant. The writers, however, included these lists because they wanted to make clear that the life and ministry of Jesus were deeply rooted in the Old Testament. The Old Testament constantly points forward to the time when God will complete his work. It is like a great musical symphony coming to a climax, but awaiting its resolution in its final and resounding chord. The Old Testament finds its resolution and climax in Jesus.

Jesus fulfils the Old Testament and points forward to God's Spirit-filled future. He called the disciples to follow him from Galilee to Jerusalem and there to prepare themselves for a new outpouring of God's Holy Spirit and the coming of his kingdom in power. In the three years of his earthly ministry, Jesus was a visual aid of what God was going to do by the power of the Holy Spirit from the day of Pentecost until Jesus comes again.

Jesus the Spirit-filled man

The power of the Spirit, hinted at in the Old Testament, became explicit in the ministry of Jesus as he ushered in God's kingdom. The one who brought the kingdom in the power of the Holy Spirit was himself a Spirit-filled person. Mark records the Old Testament prophecy (Mark 1:2–3) of the preparatory work of John the Baptist. In quick succession he tells of John's ministry, and comes immediately to the baptism of Jesus and the great words, 'You are my own dear Son' (Mark 1:11). As these words are spoken, the Spirit descends like a dove to anoint Jesus.

Matthew and Luke record these events only after they have traced the life of Jesus back to his birth and shown that, even before the anointing at his baptism, God's Spirit was present and at work. Although the Gospel of John does not record the baptism of Jesus nor the coming of the Spirit as a dove, early in the Gospel he does record another event in the life of Jesus which is perhaps just as significant.

John 2:13–21 records how Jesus made his way to the Passover in the temple at Jerusalem. Seeing the money-changers and traders, he became angry, driving them out and then debating with the religious leaders about the fall of the temple. Placed in the context of some of the insights which we discovered about the Old Testament this incident begins to take on a great significance.

The temple was divided into various courts and the selling and trading took place in the court of the Gentiles. It had been part of the original intention that the Gentiles would come into that part of the temple and catch a glimpse of the glory and power of the God of Israel. It was to be the focal point of the 'light to the Gentiles'. By their trading activity, and even more so by their dishonesty, the Jews were hiding the light and failing in their God-given mission. It was this latter fact that burned in the heart of Jesus and drove him to his dramatic action.

The debate which followed the incident was even more startling. Jesus and the religious leaders entered into a discussion about the temple and its destruction. This was not a discussion about architecture and building programmes. Jesus was making a startling claim. The glory and the Spirit of the Lord which left the temple of Jerusalem in the days of Ezekiel were returning to dwell afresh amongst men and women. No longer did God's Spirit reside in a building made with hands; he resided in the new temple—Jesus.

Day 1

Jesus: born of the Spirit

Matthew 1:18–25

This was how the birth of Jesus Christ took place. His mother Mary was engaged to Joseph, but before they were married, she found out that she was going to have a baby by the Holy Spirit. Joseph was a man who always did what was right, but he did not want to disgrace Mary publicly; so he made plans to break the engagement privately. While he was thinking about this, an angel of the Lord appeared to him in a dream and said, 'Joseph, descendant of David, do not be afraid to take Mary to be your wife. For it is by the Holy Spirit that she has conceived.' **(vv. 18–20)**

For most people today Christmas is an excuse for a period of extended celebration at the turn of the year. Any understanding of the true Christmas message has been overlaid with sentimentality and its deep wonder trivialized.

Christmas—the start of it all?

The commercial world today would have us believe that Christmas starts at the beginning of October and ends on 6 January. The key figures in the drama are a baby, some cattle, a donkey, wise men and shepherds. All this is now put together with a mixture of turkey and pantomime.

For the Gospel writers, the birth of Jesus was of great importance, deeply rooted in God's love and purpose for his world. The birth of Jesus in the stable at Bethlehem was the conclusion of many years of preparation on the part of God.

As we saw in the introduction, Matthew and Luke record the genealogical tables for us, the long lists of Jesus' ancestors. Matthew traced his list back to Abraham through the royal line of David. He emphasized that Jesus was the Messiah for whom the Jewish nation was looking and that his background equipped him for that task.

Jesus was a descendant of King David and in direct line to Abraham, the father of the covenant between God and the Jewish nation. The maker of the new covenant descended directly from the old.

Luke traced his genealogy back beyond Abraham to Adam. Through the first Adam, sin entered the world and the beauty and harmony of creation were destroyed. If the consequences of the first Adam's sin were to be put right it was then necessary for someone fully human, like Adam, to undertake the work. Jesus was fully God but, like Adam, he was also fully human.

The birth of Jesus is the focal point of all God's plans and purposes.

A very special baby

All babies are special—at least to their parents. Winston Churchill once advised that if you are not sure how to admire a particularly ugly baby simply say, 'My, that certainly is a baby!' However, the baby born in Bethlehem was special in his significance, not just for his parents, but for the history of the world and for the hope of eternal life he would bring to millions of people down the ages.

The Holy Spirit was intimately involved in the birth of Jesus. Mary and Joseph were independently challenged to see it as such. Joseph, against all his natural feelings and the pressure of social acceptance, took the pregnant Mary and made her his wife. Mary in her turn replied to the angel's message, 'I am the Lord's servant... may it happen to me as you have said' (Luke 1:38).

With a voice of singing

With the birth of Jesus it was as though a new spiritual spring burst out. The voice of prophecy, seemingly silent for many years, was again heard. God's Holy Spirit was on the move. The announcement of the birth was accompanied by prophetic outpourings of praise. Mary praised God in the words of her song (Luke 1:46–55) and these were echoed in the song of Zechariah (Luke 1:68–79).

Soon after his birth, Jesus was taken by his parents into the temple where they met the old man Simeon. Simeon was full of the Holy Spirit and open to the Spirit's prompting. Seeing this young couple coming towards him, with the small baby in the woman's arms,

Simeon suddenly recognized that God's moment had come; this was the Messiah for whom he had been longing (Luke 2:29–32). This was no human intuition but the working of the Spirit. Simeon saw that in this small, vulnerable child the kingdom of God's Spirit had dawned and light was going to fill the darkness of the nations.

Further reading

Luke 1:26–38; John 3:31–36

Pause for thought

Take time to be still and reflect on the readings and the study. Write down in your diary the one thing that has really struck you from today's study.

Pause for reflection

We celebrate Christmas as the birth of Jesus Christ. The birth of Jesus was part of God's ongoing plan to make his love known and the Spirit was intimately involved in this work. Are you willing to listen to Jesus, the one who was anointed by the Holy Spirit?

Pause for prayer

Lord Jesus, help me this week
to see you more clearly,
that I might love you more dearly
and follow you more nearly.
Amen.

John the Baptist: the ministry of the Holy Spirit

Luke 3:3–18

So John went throughout the whole territory of the River Jordan, preaching, 'Turn away from your sins and be baptized, and God will forgive your sins.' As it is written in the book of the prophet Isaiah: 'Someone is shouting in the desert: "Get the road ready for the Lord; make a straight path for him to travel! Every valley must be filled up, every hill and mountain levelled off. The winding roads must be made straight, and the rough paths made smooth. The whole human race will see God's salvation!"'

(vv. 3–6)

The years following the birth of Jesus are hardly mentioned by the Gospel writers. Indeed, only Luke records the incident of Jesus going up to the temple when he was twelve. All we know is that they were years of training and preparation and that: 'Jesus grew both in body and in wisdom, gaining favour with God and people' (Luke 2:52). However, with the beginning of John the Baptist's public ministry the pace begins to quicken and there is an air of expectation.

Act Two, Scene One

With John the Baptist it is as though the first act of God's purpose is drawing to a close. John is the last of the great Old Testament prophets, looking forward to the end of the first act and the beginning of the second in God's great drama of salvation. This is exactly how Jesus understood the ministry of John: 'For John is the one of whom the scripture says: "God said, I will send my messenger ahead of you to open the way for you." I tell you . . . John is greater than any one who has ever lived. But the one who is least in the Kingdom of God is greater than John' (Luke 7:27–28).

Jesus acknowledged the greatness of John the Baptist, indeed he suggested that John towered above the other prophets. Nevertheless, the least in the kingdom would be greater than John. At first sight this seems distinctly unfair to such a distinguished person. But Jesus was simply saying that God was doing a radical new thing in the kingdom. All those who lived before the coming of the kingdom merely looked for its day, but in Jesus the kingdom had come, and those who live after its coming are able to proclaim something far greater than John and the other prophets ever knew.

John also recognized this truth in his own teaching. He saw that he was only a signpost to the coming kingdom and that the work of Jesus was to be of far greater significance than his own: 'He must become more important while I become less important' (John 3:30).

The promise of fire

Baptism was at the heart of John's ministry. As he took men and women under the water of the Jordan, he saw their baptism as an act of repentance and preparation for the coming kingdom. It was a powerful symbol of the need for cleansing and renewal, but John recognized that the muddy waters of the Jordan could never effect a change of heart. Lives would only be transformed by the coming of the kingdom of the Messiah. The Messiah would baptize with the power of the Holy Spirit which would be like a fire cleansing the heart and lives of people and also transforming and empowering them. With John came the expectation that the kingdom of God was indeed at hand.

The coming of Jesus

It is against this background of excitement and anticipation that Jesus came and found John and asked to be baptized. At first John refused to baptize him, recognizing that *he* ought to be baptized by Jesus, the anointed one of God. However, Jesus insisted and was baptized by John. In so doing he identified himself with all those who saw their need of God. As he came up from the water, the Spirit came down like a dove, settling on him and publicly affirming his calling and his ministry—a calling which would eventually lead him to the cross where he would indeed become 'the Lamb of God, who takes away the sin of the world' (John 1:29).

Further reading

Matthew 3:1–6; Mark 1:1–15; John 1:29–34

Pause for thought

Take time to be still, allow the Lord to speak to you and then in your diary jot down the things which you feel the Holy Spirit is showing you.

Pause for reflection

Jesus is the one who baptizes with the Holy Spirit and fire. How do you feel about allowing that to happen within your life?

What is your response to the idea of being immersed in the Spirit as John immersed people in the water of the Jordan?

Pause for prayer

Lord, sometimes I am afraid
of the power of your Holy Spirit
and of what he may demand.
Give me the confidence today
to open myself to him
and to be led by him—
no matter what the consequences.
Amen.

Day 3

Jesus: temptations and the Holy Spirit

Matthew 4:1–11

Then the Spirit led Jesus into the desert to be tempted by the Devil. After spending 40 days and nights without food, Jesus was hungry. Then the Devil came to him . . . **(vv. 1–3)**

Yesterday we looked at the baptism of Jesus by John in the Jordan and the descent of the dove. The curtain was raised on the second act of God's drama and the age of his kingdom was dawning. Today we begin to trace the coming of that kingdom through the life, death and resurrection of Jesus.

The anointed one of God

The moment of Jesus' baptism was significant because it identified him with those he came to save, and marked the public affirmation of his calling by his heavenly Father. This was a confirmation of his calling and acceptance by God.

For hundreds of years the Jewish nation had been longing and looking for their Messiah, the anointed one. Jesus was the one for whom Israel was looking, the one who came in the name of the Lord and upon whom the Spirit of the Lord rested.

Compelled by the Spirit

You might have thought that as Jesus came up from the waters of Jordan his public ministry would have begun at once. Having received the public affirmation of his Father's calling, it would have seemed reasonable for Jesus immediately to preach, teach and proclaim the kingdom. This, however, was not the case. Jesus was first led into the wilderness by the Spirit to be tempted by Satan.

Throughout his life, Jesus constantly sought his Father's will and was determined to be obedient to it every step of the way. To be the anointed one meant also being the obedient one. Day by day Jesus sought his Father's guidance, as he saw the whole course of his life moving steadily and surely towards the final conflict of the cross. If we want to know what it is to be empowered by the Holy Spirit of God, we also need this willingness to walk obediently under God's direction and guiding.

Into battle!

There is a great tendency in contemporary discipleship to long for the Spirit to work in exciting and dramatic ways. Often the work of the Spirit is dramatic, but he also wants to work in secret, preparing our hearts and minds. The battle in the wilderness was specifically for the mind of Jesus, the means by which his ministry was shaped. All three temptations tried to turn him from his Father's will to seek his own ends and desires. Although anointed by the Spirit's power, he still had freedom of will to use that power for the coming of God's kingdom or the building of his own personal empire.

We still find that temptation very real today. In his sovereign will, the Lord offers us the power and gift of his Spirit, but that gift can be perverted and used to wrong ends. Thankfully for all of us, Jesus recognized the temptations for what they were and remained firm. He resisted Satan and determined to walk as prompted by the Holy Spirit, obedient to his Father's will.

Victorious for a while

Luke tells us that Satan left Jesus 'for a while'. The battle fought and won in the wilderness was only the first skirmish in the campaign. Throughout his ministry Jesus was under attack by the forces of darkness. Over and again he was tempted to turn back from the Father's calling; whether it was Peter's protestations which had to be rebuked, or in the garden of Gethsemane where he wrestled in prayer to come to the point of obedience. The final victory was only won when he hung upon the cross and in triumph declared, 'Father! In your hands I place my spirit!'

The constant openness of Jesus to the Holy Spirit had brought him through every conflict to the point of victory, not for himself but for all believers and the whole of creation.

Further reading

Luke 4:1–13

Pause for thought

Be still and quiet and allow the word of the Holy Spirit to speak to you. Fill in your diary for today.

Pause for reflection

Think about how much it cost Jesus to remain obedient to the Father's will. How would you respond to the Holy Spirit if he led you into areas of conflict?

Pause for prayer

Father, thank you for the constant obedience of Jesus.
Thank you that he was prepared
to be open to your Spirit at every point.
Please teach me the same obedience
and the same openness.
Amen.

Day 4

The Holy Spirit and the power of the kingdom

Luke 4:16–30

Then Jesus went to Nazareth, where he had been brought up, and on the Sabbath he went as usual to the synagogue. He stood up to read the Scriptures and was handed the book of the prophet Isaiah. He unrolled the scroll and found the place where it is written: 'The Spirit of the Lord is upon me, because he has chosen me to bring good news to the poor.' (vv. 16–18)

The sermon which Jesus preached in the synagogue at Nazareth is very significant and we will return to it later in our studies. Today it is important to note three things.

First, Jesus recognized his divine calling and empowering. The passage which Jesus chose from Isaiah speaks of the Lord's Messiah and servant coming in the power of the Holy Spirit. We can only imagine the stunned silence which must have followed Jesus' claim that he was fulfilling that promise.

Secondly, Jesus recognized that he ushered in God's kingdom with God's power. The kingdom that dawned with his ministry was to reverse the destructive effects of the power of sin and death. So his manifesto, laid out for him in Isaiah, was that the blind should see and those who were held in bondage for whatever reason should be set free.

These were fine words and the Gospel writers are all eager to show that they were followed up in action. The opening chapters of Mark's Gospel move forward at a breathtaking pace. He demonstrates that in Jesus the kingdom of God has not only come, but come in great power.

Within a very short space, Mark records how the sick are made whole and the dead raised. He shows that the authority of Jesus was not simply over physical illness and death. Alongside the physical healings, the possessed are set free and the powers of darkness pushed back. If this is not sufficient, he shows that Jesus has authority over the created order and wind and waves obey him. And finally to push home the point even further, he demonstrates that Jesus has the authority to forgive sins. In Jesus the kingdom had come in power, and God dwelt in human form.

In proclaiming the kingdom, Jesus did not simply demonstrate his power, but always looked for and expected a response. The kingdom brought with it the authority of the king and so Jesus called men and women to follow him. Those who recognized his authority obeyed.

A kingdom for all

The third fundamental issue is that the power of the kingdom is for all and not the selected few. Returning to the sermon at Nazareth, it is interesting to see how Jesus develops his theme. He takes the examples of the widow of Zarephath and Naaman the Syrian. Both came from the Gentile world and yet they were recipients of God's grace and blessing. Jesus claimed that the kingdom and its power were available for all.

This inclusiveness was not just for those separated by geographical boundaries. The religious leaders of Jesus' day had great lists of those who were unacceptable, including tax gatherers and prostitutes. Jesus opened the kingdom to all. By the power of God's love all are included.

The continuing conflict

The immediate response to the sermon at Nazareth was not acclaim but anger. The crowd rose up and tried to lynch Jesus. The power of the kingdom is disturbing to all who have a vested interest in maintaining the status quo. It has always been so and is certainly true today. The ultimate outcome of the conflict was, of course, the cross of Calvary. Death, though, could not hold Jesus and as the risen Lord he continues to bring his kingdom in power, calling for repentance and trust, but often finding disbelief and rejection.

Further reading

Mark 1:21–28

Pause for thought

Allow the Holy Spirit to speak to you in the silence. Write your response in your diary.

Pause for reflection

How do we recognize the kingdom that Jesus came to bring? In what ways do you believe it is a reality today, and how do you feel about it?

How does the kingdom reach out to all people? What are the implications for your discipleship today?

What does it mean to preach the kingdom in the power of the Spirit—will it still bring conflict?

Pause for prayer

Lord, forgive me when I fail to see you at work.
Help me today to recognize where you are working
so that I can cooperate with your Holy Spirit.
Amen.

Day 5

Sonship and servanthood

Mark 10:35–45

Jesus called [his disciples] together to him and said, 'You know that those who are considered rulers of the heathen have power over them, and the leaders have complete authority. This, however, is not the way it is among you. If one of you wants to be great, he must be the servant of the rest; and if one of you wants to be first, he must be the slave of all. For even the Son of Man did not come to be served; he came to serve and to give his life to redeem many people.' **(vv. 42–45)**

From his earliest years Jesus was aware of his special relationship with God as his heavenly Father. Luke tells how Jesus as a boy of twelve was left behind in Jerusalem eventually to be found in the temple. Jesus says to his parents: 'Why did you have to look for me? Didn't you know that I had to be in my Father's house?' (Luke 2:49).

The message of the angel to Mary before the birth of Jesus told of his special relationship to his heavenly Father (Luke 1:35) and this is reaffirmed by the voice of God at the moment of Jesus' baptism (Luke 3:21–22).

Born to suffer

Jesus' ministry was constantly involved in conflict. Sometimes this conflict was with human opponents—with religious leaders, or even with his family and fellow countrymen—but sometimes it was a struggle with the power of darkness. As he knew the power of the Spirit compelling him to declare the kingdom of God, so the intensity of that struggle became even greater. We might ask how Jesus had the courage and the willingness to continue.

Certainly the undergirding factor must have been the confidence and trust he had in his relationship with God as Father—something he demonstrated throughout his ministry. When he taught the disciples to pray he gave them permission to address God intimately as 'Father' (Luke 11:2). When Jesus rejoiced in the work of God he spoke to God as 'Father' (Matthew 11:25). But it was during his Passion that the intensity of this relationship was most powerfully demonstrated.

As the final act in the struggle against sin and death began, Jesus made his way to the garden of Gethsemane to pray. Left isolated and alone, aware of the great crisis which faced him, he fell on his knees in prayer struggling with the demands of God's will and yet aware that God was the Father who called him to this supreme sacrifice.

The events which followed Gethsemane, leading eventually to the cross, were simply the outworkings of the Son's willingness to be obedient to the Father's will. Even on the cross, in the midst of all the horror and pain, Jesus still knew that God was involved as his Father. He declared, 'Forgive them, Father! They don't know what they are doing' (Luke 23:34). Although there came a moment of isolation and almost despair, Jesus' final word is one of victory: 'Father! In your hands I place my spirit!' (Luke 23:46). Jesus displayed absolute confidence in his relationship with God as Father and also demonstrated that the purpose of his sonship was to come as a servant. Just as with sonship, the servanthood of Jesus finds its echoes throughout the Gospels.

Born to serve

The centurion who came to Jesus for the healing of his servant recognized that Jesus not only possessed authority but was also under authority. As with the centurion, Jesus' power was delegated from on high and had to be used correctly.

Jesus was eager to demonstrate his servant role and called his disciples to that same status. When James and John asked for the best seats in the kingdom, causing great resentment amongst the rest of the disciples, they were challenged with the role of servanthood. Jesus had authority to call others to service simply because he himself was a servant, and his life was a demonstration of that calling.

As with the sonship of Jesus, the servanthood of Jesus finds its climax and focal point in the last hours of his life. In the upper room in the face of disagreement, Jesus washed the disciples' feet. Not only is this a particular act of service, but a powerful symbol of the whole of his ministry; he came to serve and give his life, a ransom for many. The cross then becomes not a sign of defeat, but a sign of complete and utter victory—the Son has come as the servant and through his service has opened the possibility of a new relationship between God and humankind so that all might become sons and daughters of God himself.

Living in the Spirit

The birth of Jesus, his very life, was because of the work of God's Holy Spirit. Jesus could only call God 'Father' precisely because it was through the Holy Spirit that he had that relationship. Similarly, Jesus was aware that his role of servanthood sprung, not from his own thinking or intentions, but because the Holy Spirit had anointed him for that role. Jesus was quoting directly from Isaiah when he said: 'Here is my servant, whom I have chosen, the one I love, and with whom I am pleased. I will send my Spirit upon him, and he will announce judgement to the nations . . .' (Matthew 12:18–21, see Isaiah 42:1–4).

The passage which Jesus quoted is from one of the parts of Isaiah known as the Servant Songs. It expresses the longing for God's servant to come to bring freedom, reconciliation and renewal, and recognizes that this work of service could only be accomplished in the power of God's Spirit. In Jesus this prophecy finds its fulfilment.

Further reading

Matthew 12:9–21; Luke 3:21–22

Pause for thought

Be still and allow the Lord to speak. Complete your diary for today.

Pause for reflection

Jesus is the Son of God and also a servant. In what ways are you willing for the Servant King to call you into his service?

Pause for prayer

This is our God,
The Servant King,
He calls us now
To follow Him,
To bring our lives
As a daily offering
Of worship to
The Servant King.

Day 6

Jesus and the promise of the Holy Spirit

John 14:15–26

> *'If you love me, you will obey my commandments. I will ask the Father, and he will give you another Helper, who will stay with you for ever. He is the Spirit who reveals the truth about God. The world cannot receive him, because it cannot see him or know him. But you know him, because he remains with you and is in you.'* (vv. 15–17)

In the four Gospels it is Jesus who towers over everything. The writers recognize that he is the key to God's new kingdom and that he alone is able to bring about this new beginning. We have seen how Jesus was aware that it was the Spirit of God who empowered and directed him. As he spoke about the temple, about the kingdom, about his role as son and servant, Jesus dared to claim that he was the demonstration of God's Spirit, God's very presence amongst men and women. It was, and continues to be, a startling and bold claim, one which we need to grasp and understand if we are really serious about being his disciples. Only as we understand who Jesus is are we able to begin to understand who we are called to be.

Just looking and learning

The Gospels make little mention of the work of the Holy Spirit in the lives of the disciples. In many ways it seems the disciples were just spectators of all that God was doing in and through Jesus. Obviously they were drawing their own conclusions and learning about the dynamic of this new Spirit-empowered kingdom, but for the majority of the time they did not experience that power in their own lives. They did, however, have an occasional foretaste of what would become a permanent reality for them. Sent out by Jesus on a preaching mission, the disciples returned excited and rejoicing: 'The

72 men came back in great joy. "Lord" they said "even the demons obeyed us when we gave them a command in your name!" ' (Luke 10:17).

Such excitement was not the normal experience of the disciples during Jesus' lifetime. Most of the time they displayed characteristics of the world rather than of the kingdom. They were weak, unsure and in the last hours of Jesus life they betrayed him, deserted him and even denied him. After the resurrection they were still so afraid that they hid behind locked doors (John 20:19) and even wanted to return to the old life (John 21:1–3). This seems a far cry from the men and women who after the day of Pentecost turned the world upside down.

The promise of power

Jesus knew that his earthly ministry was just the beginning and the wider ministry could not come in all its fulness and potential until he had made it possible through his death and resurrection. Only then could the power of sin and death be defeated and the possibility of knowing the power of the Holy Spirit in a personal and continuing way be given to men and women. As his ministry drew to its close Jesus began to speak of the future and to talk about the promise of the Holy Spirit.

In the last meal with his disciples in the upper room he taught them about the Holy Spirit and the Spirit's significance both for believers and for the world. In his Gospel, John makes it clear that the disciples were very frightened by the sense of impending doom and confused by Jesus' words. They had no real understanding of what he was promising. Even after the resurrection it is clear that they still had no full idea of what to expect or what would happen when the Spirit came. They did, though, hold onto the promise that Jesus would send the Spirit, and the days in Jerusalem between the ascension and Pentecost were spent in expectant waiting and prayer.

Further reading

Luke 24:36–53; John 16:14–15

Pause for thought

Take time to be still and to be quiet and to ask the Lord to speak to you. Complete your diary for today.

Pause for reflection

How does the Holy Spirit transform the life of the believer?

Jesus Christ longs to fulfil his promise of the Holy Spirit in your own life. How do you respond to this truth?

Pause for prayer

Come down, O love divine,
Seek thou this soul of mine.

Bianco da Siena, tr. R.F. Littledale

Day 7

Jesus and receiving the Holy Spirit

John 7:1–10, 37–39

On the last and most important day of the festival Jesus stood up and said in a loud voice, 'Whoever is thirsty should come to me, and whoever believes in me should drink. As the scripture says, "Streams of life-giving water will pour out from his side."' Jesus said this about the Spirit, which those who believed in him were going to receive. At that time the Spirit had not yet been given, because Jesus had not been raised to glory. (vv. 37–39)

The festival to which John refers is the Feast of Tabernacles and to understand the significance of Jesus' words it is necessary to know a little bit of the background to this festival.

In this feast the people of Israel gave thanks to God for protecting them during the wanderings in the desert following the exodus. For the days of the festival many pilgrims would camp out in makeshift booths on the hills around Jerusalem. This was a reminder of the fragility of life, particularly during the time of the exodus, and the total dependence of the nation and individual upon the grace and goodness of God.

A reminder of dependence

It was also a celebration of the fact that God dwelt amongst his people as the source of their life and protection. During the exodus this dwelling was represented by the tent of the presence and as the Lord called the people to move on, so too did they move the tent. When the people settled in the Promised Land this nomadic tent of the presence was replaced by the permanence of the temple. Both symbolized that God was dwelling amongst his people in glory and power, but with the solidity of the temple came the seeds of religious decline. The Jews began to localize God into a tribal deity and move away from the truth of his sovereignty and universality.

A hope for the future

When Jesus went to Jerusalem on the last day of the Feast of Tabernacles, water was taken from the pool of Siloam and poured out in the temple. This was a symbolic reminder that when God came in power his Holy Spirit would flow from his dwelling place bringing life to every area it touched. This ritual echoed the vision of Ezekiel in which he saw the river of life flowing in an ever increasing stream from the temple (Ezekiel 47).

It was these dramatic pictures which were in Jesus' mind, and those of his hearers, when he stood up on the last day of the feast and claimed that life-giving water would flow from him. He echoed again his claim to be the new temple, God's dwelling place, but on this occasion he went one step further. He now pointed to a future when all who believed in him would not only receive the water of life, but would become a fountain of life to others. No longer would God's presence be limited to the physical temple in Jerusalem nor indeed to the one physical place where Jesus was present in his earthly body. In the future he would be present wherever his believers were gathered and there the water (the Holy Spirit) would flow.

It is not surprising that again there was conflict and division. Some believed the words, whilst others rejected them. Equally, it should not be surprising that these words continue to divide today. The words of Jesus are themselves a means of God's judgment, because they call for a response.

Further reading

John 4:13–14

Pause for thought

Take time to be still and to be quiet and to complete your diary for today.

Pause for reflection

In what ways do we use water to refresh and cleanse us? What are the lessons we can draw for our own spiritual lives?

In what ways are you prepared to allow the water of the Holy Spirit to fill you so that you can become a channel of that water for others?

Pause for prayer

River wash over me,
Cleanse me and make me new.
Bathe me, refresh me and fill me anew,
River wash over me.

Spirit watch over me,
Lead me to Jesus' feet.
Cause me to worship and fill me anew,
Spirit watch over me.

Material for group study

For sharing

As individuals within the group, note down:

◇ the things that have been new to you and enlightened you

◇ the questions that have been raised.

Divide the group into pairs and give time for each pair to share their answers.

Come together as a whole group for discussion and sharing.

For learning

Before the session the leader should prepare cards displaying various aspects of the Spirit's work in the life of Jesus.

These could be made as pieces of a jigsaw to fit together to make the whole.

Put them down one by one and discuss:

◇ their implications for Jesus

◇ their implications for the Church and disciples today.

For discussion and application

The ministry of Jesus brought with it conflict and division. Should we expect the same today and how do we deal with it?

How can we help others to discover that Jesus is God's anointed Messiah?

How do we know the power of the Spirit in our own lives and become channels for others?

For prayer

If the group is not used to praying aloud the leader could prepare cards for thanksgiving for each group member. These cards reflect the theme of the week: for example, thank you that Jesus is the anointed Messiah; thank you that by the Spirit he is the Son of God.

These could then be used in a prayer time.

Suggested prayer that can be prayed together or by the leader:

Heavenly Father,
thank you for the work of the Spirit
in the life of Jesus.
Thank you for all that Jesus showed us of you
and for the kingdom he came to bring.
Help us day by day to see more of your truth,
know more of your kingdom
and live more fully in the power of your Spirit,
as Jesus did.
Amen.

WEEK 3

THE HOLY SPIRIT IN THE NEW TESTAMENT

Whilst, in many ways, our present world is far removed from the world of the first-century Christian Church, there are also some remarkable similarities. The Church was born into a world which was both multi-cultural and multi-faith. Some of those faiths and religions were established with many adherents. It was also a time of a proliferation of sects and every possible expression of religious belief.

This is very much like our own day. We live in a multi-cultural, multi-faith society, and, as we draw to the end of the millennium, every religious 'crackpot' will be peddling his wares.

The early Church was also in a mission situation. Sometimes this was exciting, but frequently the world was hostile to the gospel. In our own nation, as in many others, we too are now in a mission situation. No longer can it be assumed that anyone knows anything about the Christian faith, and church culture becomes more and more alien to the majority around us.

For that early Church there were no clear markers. The Christians simply had a wide agenda to preach the gospel to all nations and a sure promise that the Lord was with them and would give them the power of his Spirit.

The course ahead was uncharted, but they found themselves willing to launch out into the unknown, prepared to go as and when the Spirit led. In the present day, many of the familiar landmarks within church life are either no longer there or fast disappearing. Many Christians today feel afraid of the future because once again the way is uncharted.

It is into this situation that the Spirit of God wishes to blow afresh. In the pages of the New Testament we discover principles to encourage us and to equip us.

Principles and examples

It has been said quite rightly, that the Acts of the Apostles is not intended to be a teaching book. It is much more a narrative telling the story of the early Church. This being so, it would be inappropriate to seek out great principles from its pages and relate them to today's Church. The New Testament letters are the place to discover the principles, as Church leaders reflected on what the Spirit had been doing, drew conclusions and laid down the teaching. One of the fascinating features of the Acts is that the Christians themselves were frequently surprised by what the Lord was doing and spent their time catching up with the Holy Spirit as he led the mission of the Church from one place to the next.

The book of Acts provides important examples which give clear insights into the working of the Holy Spirit. The power which he brings, the direction he gives, the unity he builds, the transformation he effects are all important features of the book, features which are amplified elsewhere in the New Testament. Because our God is the same yesterday, today and for ever, it is important to look at his work in the Acts of the Apostles and to allow it to become a mirror for the contemporary Church. Today's Church needs to discover afresh the breath of God to empower it in mission and ministry.

Dynamite, wind and fire

The Greek word for 'power' is *dunamis* from which is derived the English word 'dynamite'. The Spirit is about the reality of God's power breaking into the lives of individuals and God's new community, the Church. The symbols chosen by God to show the power of the Spirit were wind and fire, two of the most powerful forces in the world, which can either be harnessed for good and constructive purposes or can wreak havoc and destruction. It is crucial to recognize that the power of God's Holy Spirit is neither impersonal nor mindless. He comes from the heart of God himself and is given to the Church by the risen and glorified Jesus. The Spirit may bring all the power of dynamite, might blow like a mighty hurricane and burn like a fierce fire, but his power can be trusted because it flows from the loving heart of God.

Some important warnings

Because the Spirit comes from the holy and sovereign God the Acts of the Apostles contains serious warnings about the way in which we should approach him. Acts 5 contains the sad and sorry tale of Ananias and Sapphira. This couple sold property for the good of the Church but kept back part of the proceeds for themselves. Their sin was lying—pretending to give all when in fact this was not the case. Peter observes in Acts 5:3, 'Ananias, why did you let Satan take control of you and make you lie to the Holy Spirit by keeping part of the money you received for the property?' and again in verse 9 of the same chapter Peter asks of Sapphira, 'Why did you and your husband decide to put the Lord's Spirit to the test?' God's Holy Spirit is not to be mocked; it is a serious matter dealing with the holy God and demands integrity and honesty.

The second warning comes in chapter 8 and concerns a magician called Simon. Having astounded the Samaritans with his occult practices Simon met Peter and John and saw the Holy Spirit come down upon the Samaritans. He was so impressed that he offered the apostles money to buy the gift of the Spirit. Peter immediately rounded on him and condemned such an attitude. Whilst our experience may not parallel Simon's exactly, it is a timely reminder that the Spirit is not our plaything. Our hearts need to be right with God.

As well as the warnings, as we read the Acts of the Apostles, we sense something of the excitement and anticipation of that early Church as they set out on the missionary task, empowered by God's Holy Spirit.

Day 1

The promise of power

Acts 1:1–8

Jesus said to them, 'The times and occasions are set by my Father's own authority, and it is not for you to know when they will be. But when the Holy Spirit comes upon you, you will be filled with power, and you will be witnesses for me in Jerusalem, in all Judea and Samaria, and to the ends of the earth.' (vv. 7–8)

When the disciples gathered for their last meal with Jesus there must have been a sense of impending doom. They did not fully realize that it was to be the last time they would be together in this way, nor did they appreciate its significance. They must, though, have been aware that events were coming to a climax. They had witnessed the growing tension since his triumphal entry into Jerusalem. Some hoped that Jesus was about to act decisively to bring in the kingdom, but others were more concerned for his safety and feared the authorities. Whilst they did not believe he would allow events to get out of control, they also remembered that he had foretold his suffering and death in Jerusalem. The storm clouds were indeed gathering and they knew they faced an uncertain future.

Power for renewal

Recognizing this sense of uncertainty and fear, Jesus talked to them about the Holy Spirit. The disciples had witnessed the many things Jesus had said and done. They had been amazed at the authority they seemed to possess when he had sent them out to declare the good news of the kingdom. They had also known times of weakness and failure, and were aware that they knew little of the power of the kingdom in a deep, personal way.

In the upper room, the disciples could not bear to think of Jesus going away; they had little or no realization of what it meant. However, in the months to come, they would remember their last meal together, and the conversation with Jesus. They would discover his promise of the Holy Spirit becoming a reality in their own lives and personal experience, and they would understand the meaning and significance which lay behind his words.

Power for the world

Jesus promised that the Holy Spirit was going to be of far greater importance than simply enabling the disciples to 'feel good'. The Spirit was also going to work beyond the lives of the disciples, and indeed beyond the confines of the Church. He would be at work in the world, convincing men and women of their need of repentance, and helping them to see the centrality of Jesus Christ. Jesus had opened the way for the kingdom of God to dawn. Having fulfilled his earthly ministry, he would continue his work by the power of the Holy Spirit and in cooperation with the disciples.

Power for witness

Having made all these promises, Jesus went from the supper table to Gethsemane, to the cross, eventually to the glory of the resurrection, to meeting with the disciples on the day of the ascension, and finally to sit at God's right hand. Although the disciples met with the risen Lord on numerous occasions after his resurrection, very little changed. They were still frightened and uncertain. They demanded to know dates and times. Like us, they demanded such detail, because it made them feel safe and secure. It was as though the miracle of the resurrection was not sufficient. They craved more and more. The truth is that no matter how much knowledge Jesus might have given them, in itself it would not have been enough. They needed transformation from within. The external reality of the resurrection had to become an inner certainty.

Jesus knew he could not give precise details of time and place. He did, however, promise that they would receive power, and that would be sufficient. This power would not be to keep for their own pleasure and amusement, but to enable them to be witnesses—in their own known territory, across the border in unfriendly Samaria, and then across every border to the ends of the earth.

Power until the end of the age

The age of the Spirit will come to an end when Jesus returns. The victory which was won on the cross and through the resurrection will have its final triumph when Jesus Christ returns as Lord. The work of the Holy Spirit will continue to prepare for and point to that day.

Jesus promised that his disciples would receive the baptism of the Holy Spirit, as John the Baptist had foretold. John had baptized by immersing people in the river Jordan. They had been engulfed by the water, taken right into the current of the river. The parallels should be clear. The promise of Jesus is that his followers will know the power of the Spirit like the current of a mighty river, engulfing their lives. His disciples must be prepared to entrust themselves to the buoyancy of the Spirit, and to be carried where he flows.

This was to be the experience of the early Church and it is to be our experience. The God of the New Testament is the same God who meets us today, who longs to equip us, and baptize us by his Spirit.

Further reading

John 14:15–17; 16:4b–15

Pause for thought

In the silence try and imagine you are with the disciples in the upper room sharing the Last Supper. Listen to the words of Jesus as though for the first time. Think about the promise of the Holy Spirit and the implications of that promise for your life today. Write your conclusions in your diary.

Pause for reflection

How do we recognize the work of the Holy Spirit in our lives?

In what ways can you ask to be carried along by the flow of the river of the Spirit—to be immersed in his life?

Do you hold back and if so why?

Pause for prayer

Lord, the power of your Holy Spirit
is like a mighty river.
Help me to entrust myself
to the current of his flow.
Sometimes your promises seem too big
and ask too much.
Help me to know
that your promises can be trusted
because you are the God of love.
Amen.

Day 2

The coming of power

Acts 2:1–13

When the day of Pentecost came, all the believers were gathered together in one place. Suddenly there was a noise from the sky which sounded like a strong wind blowing, and it filled the whole house where they were sitting. Then they saw what looked like tongues of fire which spread out and touched each person there. They were all filled with the Holy Spirit and began to talk in other languages, as the Spirit enabled them to speak. (vv. 1–4)

For many Christians the day of Pentecost and its meaning and promise is still a closed book. This is despite the growth of the charismatic movement in the past thirty or so years, when more and more have discovered the significance of God the Holy Spirit in their lives and in the life of the local church.

As a young child I can remember understanding Christmas and realizing that God had sent Jesus into the world. I knew that Good Friday and Easter Sunday were about the cross and the resurrection and that Jesus had died for me. I was however very confused about Pentecost, or Whit Sunday as it was then called. No one ever explained its purpose to me and the only explanation seemed to be that an aged aunt came to stay with us and it was always half term (it was not until I was nineteen that I came to understand the person and work of God the Holy Spirit more fully).

The story so far

The previous weeks' studies have shown that God the Holy Spirit was an integral part of the work of the Trinity from the very beginning of creation. Throughout the Old Testament he acted in the lives of individuals and situations, and the Old Testament was always looking for the time when he would come in all his fulness. That time arrived with the birth of Jesus. He was anointed with the

Holy Spirit who empowered every aspect of his ministry. In every way Jesus fulfilled the longings of the Old Testament. This fulfilment, however, applied to the promises about the Messiah, but did not apply to the promises concerning the Holy Spirit in the lives of individual men and women.

A promise for everyone

Towards the end of the Old Testament the prophets longed for the Spirit to renew the hearts of men and women so they might keep close to the Lord in their willingness to obey him. They also looked for the time when the Spirit might not be the prerogative of the few but the experience of the many. On the day of Pentecost this promise was finally fulfilled.

Following the ascension, Jesus' disciples obediently returned to Jerusalem and awaited the promised power of the Holy Spirit. They had little or no idea what this promise really meant or how it would manifest itself. It is also very probable that they were still afraid for their safety and were quite glad not to have to begin a public ministry. They were weak, ineffective and unready for any great task or mission. The Holy Spirit transformed the lives of those early disciples and, through their witness, brought the promise of God's Spirit to all people everywhere.

Signs of power

It is no coincidence that God chose signs of great elemental power to demonstrate the coming of the Spirit. The forces of wind and fire were a vivid demonstration of the power which became available to men and women with the coming of the Holy Spirit. The wind that blew was no gentle evening breeze, calming and bringing a sense of contentment and ease. This was a mighty hurricane blowing all before it. Travelling through South-East England after the hurricane of 1987 demonstrated to me just how powerful wind can be. Fire is equally powerful—there is nothing more terrifying than seeing a great forest blaze consuming all in its path.

It could be said that wind and fire are forces that are both impersonal and destructive, and therefore inappropriate symbols for the power of the personal Spirit of God. The Holy Spirit is the very nature of the sovereign God who is love and so we have no need to be afraid of him, however he manifests himself to us. Indeed we dishonour him if we try to deny his power.

Signs of the Spirit

The Holy Spirit came to those first believers while they were together in one place. So often discipleship has been expressed in terms of the individual in isolation. Indeed, some still talk of 'making my communion'. Whilst discipleship must begin with an individual's relationship with the Lord Jesus Christ, discipleship was never intended to be solitary. Throughout the scriptures God longs to relate to and create community. The Spirit's job is to weld and mould individuals into a caring, sharing community. The group were together in their weakness and together they discovered the power of God as the Spirit came upon them.

A further sign of the coming of the Spirit was the gift of tongues. Tongues were given so that all could hear them speaking in their own languages about the great things God had done. The Holy Spirit gives individual gifts to Christians so that the ministry of the Church might be empowered to point away from itself to Jesus Christ, and to proclaim clearly all that he has done.

Further reading

Joel 2:28–32

Pause for thought

In the silence think about the two great symbols of wind and fire. Are you willing to allow the Holy Spirit to blow into your life and burn in your heart?

Write down your response in your diary. Don't be afraid to express how you really feel.

Pause for reflection

The Holy Spirit comes from the God who loves you more than you realize. If you feel afraid of the power of the Holy Spirit can you identify why? Are you able to say 'yes' to the gift God wants to give you?

Pause for prayer

Lord, forgive me for the times
I have been afraid of your Holy Spirit.
Teach me again of your love,
and give me the courage
to open myself today
to the wind and fire of your Spirit.
Amen.

The Holy Spirit and community

Acts 2:42–47

They spent their time in learning from the apostles, taking part in the fellowship, and sharing in the fellowship meals and the prayers.

(v. 42)

God has always been eager to share in a relationship with his creation. This relationship was not only to have implications for the way God and human beings live together, but also for the way in which human beings deal with each other.

The great laws of the Old Testament were concerned not only with the 'vertical' relationship between God and humankind, but also in the 'horizontal' relationship between one human being and another. Jesus summed up the great commandment that 'You shall love the Lord your God with all your heart, with all your soul, with all your mind, and with all your strength' by adding, 'love your neighbour as yourself'.

A people for the Lord

This two-dimensional relationship seems straightforward and obvious. It must be right for human beings to be at one with their Creator and each other. From the beginning God longed for a community to be in relationship with him so that his glory might be seen in the world; this was his desire for the Jewish nation. They were to be holy, set apart, so that the holy God might be recognized and worshipped by the surrounding nations. God's longing in the New Testament is no different. In John 17, Jesus prays that the disciples, and those who come after, might be one, just as he and the Father are one. At the heart of creation is the community of the Trinity—Father, Son and Holy Spirit. It is God's desire, and Jesus' prayer, that the Christian Church might reflect that unity and community.

This is the emphasis behind Paul's words: 'Do your best to preserve the unity which the Spirit gives by means of the peace that binds you together' (Ephesians 4:3).

Paul wants Christians to be at one, not because it is a good idea, or because it is better to live at peace rather than in conflict, but because the Church needs to reflect the very nature of God in the unity and community in which it lives and displays.

A new community

These are fine sounding words, reflecting the desire of God as revealed in the Bible. Acts 2 puts the flesh, the reality, onto the theological bones. The effect of the outpouring of the Holy Spirit on the day of Pentecost was to call the Church into being—to be a community demonstrating the power of God himself. Such a community was not simply God's desire for the first century, it is his longing for his people in every generation. Acts 2 makes clear what God wants for his people by the power of the Holy Spirit.

'They learnt from the apostles'. The Holy Spirit gave both an ability to preach and teach and also a desire to listen and to learn. Sadly, in so many churches today both the ability and the desire are missing. For the Church to meet the demands of our present generation and to proclaim Jesus Christ, it is necessary for Church members to be eager to learn and for those who teach to do so by the power of the Holy Spirit.

'They took part in the fellowship'. It has been said that so often Christians organize many meetings but have no true meeting. True relationship with Jesus Christ means true relationship with our fellow Christians with a deep love and concern one for another. Such a love and concern cannot be generated by our own wills, it has to be given to us as a gift of the Holy Spirit. It is a sad fact that there are many people in our nation today who have been hindered in their search for the Christian faith because of the lack of love and fellowship they have experienced within the Christian Church. This is not only a tragedy it is also a travesty of what God wants. Church communities are meant to be places of warm acceptance where healing and wholeness can flourish. The Spirit must blow afresh in our congregations and churches to bring this true fellowship.

'The fellowship meals'. While closely related to fellowship, fellowship meals underline the New Testament commitment to hospitality. To eat a meal together can be a true expression of fellowship and community. Some think the fellowship meal here is the Eucharist. Whether or not that is the case, there is a sense in which every meal should be sacramental for the Christian disciple. Christ is present and his Holy Spirit longs to bring us together around the table.

'The prayers'. The heart of any church congregation must be its prayer life. The early Christians discovered the power of prayer and, furthermore, the Lord who answers prayer. Wherever the Spirit is allowed to lead the community of God's people he will be building a community centred on prayer.

The rest of Acts 2 and the passage from Acts 6 earth this community which the Spirit longed to build even more firmly in the real world. In Acts 2:44–46 we read how the early Christians shared their belongings one with another. This is often written off as a failed attempt to live a true communal life. But, as elsewhere, there is a stress on real commitment one to another, caring for each other's needs and sharing each other's riches. The privatization of the individual has no part in the Christian Church. The Spirit wants to break down barriers and to help Christians recognize their responsibility to each other and their mutual interdependence.

Further reading

Acts 6:1–7; Ephesians 4

Pause for thought

What are the main issues which are raised by today's study? What are the challenges to you as an individual and are there challenges for your local church? Write down your responses in your diary.

Pause for reflection

Why does the community life of the Church today often seem so far from the picture in the New Testament?

How can we encourage each other to allow the Holy Spirit to build his community and fellowship amongst us?

Pause for prayer

Lord, we dare to ask
that you will take our individual lives
and make us into the community you want us to be.
Amen.

Day 4

The Holy Spirit setting course for the future

Acts 13:1–12

While they were serving the Lord and fasting, the Holy Spirit said to them, 'Set apart for me Barnabas and Saul, to do the work to which I have called them.' (v. 2)

Throughout the book of Acts there is an awareness that God is in control, guiding and directing his Church by the power of the Holy Spirit. The author of the book, Luke, sees the Acts of the Apostles as the second part of God's work. In his Gospel, Luke shows us the ways in which the Holy Spirit anointed and then guided and prompted Jesus. In the Acts of the Apostles, Luke shows us that the risen and ascended Lord gave the gift of the Holy Spirit to his body, the Church, in order that his work might continue. The kingdom which he had come to proclaim would go on being proclaimed through the Church and by the power of the same Spirit.

Opening up the horizons

In Acts 1, Jesus promised that the power of the Holy Spirit would lead the apostles from Jerusalem to the ends of the earth via Judea and Samaria. In chapter 2, with the coming of the Holy Spirit, Luke tells how the promise of Jesus is fulfilled. The gospel is indeed preached first in Jerusalem, and then to Samaria and the final chapters find Paul in Rome, the very heart of the empire, ready to defend himself and to proclaim the kingdom at the very seat of imperial power. Throughout, the thrust and direction is not determined by the individual apostles but by the Lord himself, who through his Holy Spirit, guides and gives direction.

Open to the way of the Lord

So often the contemporary Church seems to take little notice of the voice of the Holy Spirit, relying rather on its own intuition and wisdom. This denies the principles laid down in scripture. We have already seen that throughout the vast sweep of the Old Testament, God was at work preparing the way for the final fulfilment of his revelation. Likewise in the Gospels, Jesus knew the leading of the Spirit from the moment of his birth right through to the moment of his final victory on the cross.

So it must be for the Church, if it is to be truly an instrument for God's mission to his world; it cannot live for itself or by itself. At all points the Church has to be empowered by the Holy Spirit, for he alone can reveal the mind of God and make clear the direction his Church must take. He alone can enable God's people to set course for the future. Fundamentally the Spirit calls the Church to share the missionary heart of God.

Learning to know the Lord's guidance

There are four fundamental principles which are at work as the Spirit calls us to set course for the future, willing to be blown by his wind and carried in the current of his flow:

A word from the Lord. In today's key verse the prophets declared God's word to the Church and called for Barnabas and Saul to be set aside for the work of mission. A further example of prophetic ministry comes in Acts 11:27–29, when the prophet Agabus foretells a severe famine: 'About that time some prophets went from Jerusalem to Antioch. One of them, named Agabus, stood up and by the power of the Spirit predicted that a severe famine was about to come over all the earth. (It came when Claudius was emperor.) The disciples decided that they would each send as much as they could to help their fellow-believers who lived in Judea.'

The early Church was very aware that the Lord spoke to his people and gave direction and guidance through the ministry of prophecy. Prophecy has, of course, always been notoriously difficult to assess. From the early times of the Old Testament the question was asked as to how you could distinguish a true prophet from a false one (Deuteronomy 18:21). One answer was to see if the prophecy came true. The problem was that the period between prophecy and fulfilment was often longer than one generation. It was then very difficult to see whether a prophecy was fulfilled. The other test of prophecy was to see whether the prophet's word, and indeed his character, were in accord with the revealed truths of scripture. This was and must be a continuing criterion.

Within the early Church the gift of prophecy was accepted and used. The word came through worship, prayer and fasting. The early Church must have tried and tested the prophetic word and were then willing to act upon it.

Direction. From the day of Pentecost the early Church was under the direction of the risen Jesus, mediated by the Holy Spirit. The journey of the Christian faith from Jerusalem to Rome and from its Jewish background to a pagan world was not haphazard and purposeless. Every move forward was under the Lord's guidance. Peter crossed the boundaries from Jew to Gentile as he visited Cornelius (Acts 10). Philip did likewise as he was sent to the Ethiopian eunuch (Acts 8:26–39). On another occasion Paul and his party were prevented from going in one direction by God's Spirit (Acts 16:7). Instead they found themselves called to Macedonia. This dynamic of the Spirit was the norm and expected. It should be the eager expectation of the Church and the individual disciple today.

Growth. It has been said when Church leaders in the West gather together they ask each other, 'How are things going?' They never dare to ask, 'How are things growing?' In the West we have come to expect that our churches will not grow significantly and that we are very much in a holding operation. Such a picture is not true of the world Church today, nor is it the picture of the New Testament. The Church then expected and saw growth, as do many parts of the contemporary world Church, 'And every day the Lord added to their group those who were being saved' (Acts 2:47). In Acts 6:7 we read: 'The word of God continued to spread. The number of disciples in Jerusalem grew larger and larger.'

The clue to this growth is given in Acts 9:31: 'And so it was that the church throughout Judea, Galilee, and Samaria had a time of peace.

Through the help of the Holy Spirit it was strengthened and grew in numbers, as it lived in reverence for the Lord.'

The growth of the Church was not the result of the apostles' hard work, although they did labour faithfully, nor was it the work of carefully planned mission strategies, although they did follow the strategies given to them by the Spirit. The Church grew because the Holy Spirit strengthened it and gave the increase. Again there must be lessons here for our churches today.

Warning. The Spirit needs to be obeyed! We have already seen in Acts 16:7 that Paul was prevented by the Spirit from entering the province of Bithynia. In Acts 20:22–23 Luke records part of Paul's farewell sermon to the Ephesian elders: 'And now, in obedience to the Holy Spirit I am going to Jerusalem, not knowing what will happen to me there. I only know that in every city the Holy Spirit has warned me that prison and troubles wait for me.'

The world in which the Church is set has always been, and continues to be, hostile to the word of God. It is crucial that the Church and individual Christians are willing to listen to the promptings of the Holy Spirit. He may prevent them from entering one situation or encourage them to go to another, recognizing that opposition will face them. In fighting the battles it is paramount that they are fought on grounds and in ways determined by God's Holy Spirit. We dare not set out without his guidance and direction.

Pause for thought

What are the things that prevent you from hearing the voice of God's Holy Spirit guiding and directing you? Write down these and other thoughts in your diary.

Pause for reflection

It has been said of most churches that if the work of the Holy Spirit was removed 95 per cent of their programme would continue. Is this true of your church? If so why? Are there positive observations you can make?

Pause for prayer

Lord, help us as your Church
to be open to the leading of your Holy Spirit.
Teach us how to hear his voice,
discern his truth
and walk in his power.
Amen.

Day 5

The Holy Spirit and facing the world

Acts 4:23–31

As soon as Peter and John were set free, they returned to their group and told them what the chief priests and the elders had said. When the believers heard it, they all joined together in prayer to God: '... And now, Lord, take notice of the threats they have made, and allow us, your servants, to speak your message with all boldness. Stretch out your hand to heal, and grant that wonders and miracles may be performed through the name of your holy Servant Jesus.' **(vv. 23–24, 29–30)**

Within a very short while of the coming of the Holy Spirit the Church faced persecution. At the very heart of creation there is enmity against God the Creator. This enmity can show itself in many different forms, but always it will speak against the Spirit of God.

A story of opposition

In the Old Testament, when the Spirit inspired the prophets to speak God's word, they soon found themselves facing opposition. Indeed, Jeremiah was warned at the time of his call that he would face a solid wall of opposition.

This opposition to the prophets, and the Lord's Spirit within them, becomes focused in its intensity in the ministry of Jesus. It has already been seen that with the coming of the Spirit at his baptism, Jesus was led not to an acclaimed public ministry but into the wilderness to be tempted by Satan. It is as though the Spirit is saying that ministry in his power is about confrontation with the powers of Satan and darkness.

With the return from the wilderness, Jesus' public ministry was worked out on the anvil of opposition. Luke records how, following

Jesus' first sermon, the crowds tried to lynch him. Mark tells how the Pharisees met with the Herodians and made plans to kill Jesus.

The rest of the gospel story is, of course, the gradual move towards the cross and the final conflict with human and spiritual powers. From the debates with the Pharisees, the struggle in the garden of Gethsemane, and the final conflict upon the cross, it is clear that Jesus knew that the Holy Spirit was showing him that the way of suffering was the way the Father had willed.

The call of the cross

At the heart of discipleship lies the cross. The cross is the means by which God redeemed creation and made salvation and new life possible for humankind. However, whilst Christians believe that the work of the cross was once and for all, it is important to recognize that the shadow of the cross falls over the centuries from the victory of Calvary until the Lord's coming again in glory. Something of the struggle of the cross will continue in the life of the Church and the individual Christian until the Lord returns. Those who seek to walk in the power of the Holy Spirit will find that he calls them over and over again to walk the way of the cross, the way of suffering. For those who are the Lord's, and know the power of the Holy Spirit, there will be the inevitability of opposition and the possibility of suffering.

So much of Christian culture today wants to follow current contemporary culture that demands life is pleasant and easy. Self-fulfilment and self-realization is the name of the game. It is a very real trap for Christians. Some expect the Holy Spirit to be the divine panacea who will make everything comfortable and take all the threat and pressure out of discipleship. Nothing can be further from the truth. Those who are led by the Holy Spirit will find themselves confronting the powers of darkness. Those who seek to live at the frontiers of Christian discipleship will soon find themselves in conflict with the powers of this present age.

Wrestling against the principalities and powers

Recent years have seen a stress on the more dramatic manifestations of this conflict with the powers of darkness. This may be because as a generation we demand the dramatic and spectacular. There is, of course, the place for exorcism and the direct confrontation with Satan's power, but his hold is just as significant in the more mundane structures of our lives. The dishonesty in business practice, the tensions in family life, the exploitation and marginalization of millions of people are all signs of the kingdom of Satan. The Holy Spirit anointed Jesus to proclaim the kingdom and the same Spirit now empowers God's people to proclaim the same kingdom in his name. This is the discipleship to which we are called and inevitably it is a direct challenge to those who wish to preserve the existing order.

Dangerous discipleship

Peter and John were arrested for speaking the name of Jesus: 'Peter said to [the lame man], "I have no money at all, but I give you what I have: in the name of Jesus Christ of Nazareth I order you to get up and walk!"' (Acts 3:6).

The Holy Spirit gave them a confidence to speak out in the name of Jesus and they refused to desist from this. They said: 'You yourselves judge which is right in God's sight—to obey you or to obey God. For we cannot stop speaking of what we ourselves have seen and heard' (Acts 4:19–20). Peter and John's example must be a foundation principle for the Church today. The centre of our teaching and proclamation must be the person of Jesus Christ.

Their response to opposition was to meet together. There will, of course, be times when opposition has to be borne individually, but God wants the community of his people to share together. It is to the congregation that the Spirit speaks. The congregation recognized the threat of opposition, but they also recognized that the power of the Lord was greater. They prayed that that power would be given to them afresh, that they might be willing to speak, despite the threat of opposition. If we live in isolation, there is a great danger that things can fall out of perspective. We shall take on an embattled mentality which will mean that we shall withdraw from facing the opposition. The early Church discovered the Spirit came to them afresh and compelled them to proclaim God's word. They sought the Lord's blessing that they might speak the word with all boldness. So often the Church looks to its own resources and strength. The root of the conflict is of a spiritual nature and can only be fought with spiritual weapons, given by the Spirit.

They expected the Lord to act with power and that the signs of the kingdom would be made manifest in the name of Jesus. It is at this point that the Spirit took the initiative. We are told: 'When they finished praying, the place where they were meeting was shaken. They were all filled with the Holy Spirit and began to proclaim God's message with boldness' (Acts 4:31).

If the Church today is to be vibrant and active, it is vital that we allow the Holy Spirit again to take the initiative, to fill our lives and to give us the power to proclaim God's message with all necessary boldness.

Pause for thought

In what ways do you see the spiritual battle around you? Jot down your answers in your diary.

Pause for reflection

What part does your membership of the local church play in helping you to stand firm in the face of opposition?

Pause for prayer

Lord, we pray that
in the power of your Spirit
you will shake your Church again
that we might be filled by your Spirit
and proclaim your message with boldness.
Amen.

Day 6

The Holy Spirit and proclaiming the kingdom

Acts 2:36–41

> *'All the people of Israel, then, are to know for sure that this Jesus, whom you crucified, is the one that God has made Lord and Messiah!' When the people heard this, they were deeply troubled and said to Peter and the other apostles, 'What shall we do, brothers?' Peter said to them, 'Each one of you must turn away from your sins and be baptized in the name of Jesus Christ, so that your sins will be forgiven; and you will receive God's gift, the Holy Spirit.'* **(vv. 36–38)**

The kingdom proclaimed by the early Church was no different from that proclaimed by Jesus. As during his earthly ministry Jesus was the key to open the door of the kingdom, so it was with the coming of the Spirit. The early Christians were aware that they had nothing and could do nothing of themselves; they could only rely on the Holy Spirit to point them to Jesus Christ.

So Peter says to the lame man: 'I have no money at all, but I give you what I have: in the name of Jesus Christ of Nazareth I order you to get up and walk!' (Acts 3:6).

So Philip tells the Ethiopian the good news about Jesus: 'Then Philip began to speak; starting from this passage of scripture, he told him the Good News about Jesus' (Acts 8:35).

So the whole focus of Paul's teaching is on the person of Jesus.

Some important conclusions

An overview of the Acts of the Apostles leads to four conclusions. First, there is the centrality of Jesus Christ. Jesus himself promised that when the Holy Spirit came he would not glorify himself but rather Jesus. The Spirit is given that Jesus might be made known (John 16:13–14).

Secondly, there is the prominence of the Old Testament in the preaching of the early Church. It featured strongly in Peter's sermon on the day of Pentecost and again when he spoke to Cornelius (Acts 10). It was the thrust of Stephen's defence before his execution (Acts 7) and it occurred regularly in the preaching and teaching of Paul. The Old Testament was the scripture available to the early Church and so they turned to it for their authority and mandate.

Thirdly, there is a great expectation that the Spirit is going to be at work. The book of Acts is a record of remarkable events, from healings to timely earthquakes, but the stress over and again was not on the events themselves, but on the work of Jesus Christ upon the cross. The gospel is about the means by which God has made it possible for us to be put right with him. Amidst all the excitement and expectation this was seen as the fundamental miracle, that God had provided the means of salvation.

Finally, the early Church never became bound by doctrine and dogma. The past was relevant and alive simply because the Holy Spirit was at work in the present moment, and the Holy Spirit was expected to be at work in the present because of all that God had done in the past in preparation. In the early Church there was a true coming together of the proclaiming of the word and the power of the Spirit.

This must be a challenge to the contemporary Church and to each of us in our discipleship. The proclamation of the cross of Jesus Christ must be shot through with an expectation that his Holy Spirit will be at work in the present moment, pointing only to Jesus. Those who look for the work of the Holy Spirit must recognize that any authentic sign of his power will be deeply rooted in the cross and resurrection of Jesus.

Further reading

Acts 5:12–16; Acts 19:1–10

Pause for thought

What does it mean to be deeply rooted in the cross of Christ? Jot down your reactions in your diary.

Pause for reflection

Jesus is the full revelation of God to the world. In what ways are you prepared for Jesus to be the focal point of your witness and life?

Pause for prayer

Lord, send me out
in the power of your Spirit
to proclaim the kingdom of the Lord Jesus Christ
and to inspire others to work for your glory.
Amen.

Go in peace to love and serve the Lord.
In the name of Christ
Amen.

Day 7

The Holy Spirit and the changing of lives

Acts 9:1–19

There was a believer in Damascus named Ananias. He had a vision, in which the Lord said to him, 'Ananias!' 'Here I am, Lord,' he answered. The Lord said to him, 'Get ready and go to Straight Street, and at the house of Judas ask for a man from Tarsus named Saul. He is praying, and in a vision he has seen a man named Ananias come in and place his hands on him so that he might see again.' Ananias answered, 'Lord, many people have told me about this man and about all the terrible things he has done to your people in Jerusalem. And he has come to Damascus with authority from the chief priests to arrest all who worship you.' The Lord said to him, 'Go, because I have chosen him to serve me, to make my name known to Gentiles and kings and to the people of Israel. And I myself will show him all that he must suffer for my sake.' **(vv. 10–16)**

Our God is in the business of changing lives and in the Acts of the Apostles we see that this is an important part of the Holy Spirit's work. From beginning to end, the book of Acts is a record of transformation. Men and women held enthralled to evil and Satan are set free. Those whose hearts were hardened against the truth find a new softness entering their soul. Those who regarded themselves as outsiders are found and invited to come into the Lord's family. It is a remarkable testimony to the power of God to change lives and situations.

Transformed lives

The frightened men and women who met in the upper room on the day of Pentecost discovered the power to proclaim openly the Lordship of Jesus Christ and to begin to turn the world upside down. Peter is a particularly good example of this transforming power. It was Peter who ran to the tomb with John on the first Easter Sunday and found it empty, and subsequently met the risen Jesus on numerous occasions. It was the same Peter who, even after he had met the risen Jesus, wanted to return to his old life as a fisherman. The resurrection as such made very little difference either to him or the other disciples. It was not until the power and reality of the resurrection burned into their hearts and lives that they were able to begin the true work of ministry and preaching.

When I was at school in the early days of my Christian discipleship, my tutor, an ardent atheist, would often discuss the merits of Christianity. The only point he would ever concede is that something 'must have happened to change the lives of people like Peter'. That 'something' was of course the Holy Spirit on the day of Pentecost.

The story of Saul of Tarsus is another example of the transforming power of God's Holy Spirit. From a man who 'kept up violent threats of murder against the followers of the Lord' Saul, or Paul as he later called himself, was to become the one of whom the Lord said 'I have chosen him to serve me, to make my name known to Gentiles and kings and to the people of Israel'. The Holy Spirit is always transforming lives and situations.

Can we analyse what is happening in the transformation? The answer is 'yes' and the book of Acts shows four pointers to this process of change.

The end of inner warfare

In his defence before King Agrippa in Acts 26, Paul tells the story of his conversion experience. In verse 14 there is a significant statement: 'All of us fell to the ground, and I heard a voice say to me in Hebrew, "Saul, Saul! Why are you persecuting me? You are hurting yourself by hitting back, like an ox kicking against its owner's stick."' Paul himself admitted that there had been a tremendous battle of conscience and will taking place in his heart and mind while he was involved in persecuting the Church.

The vibrancy of the young Christian community had both challenged and disturbed Paul. He had witnessed and approved the murder of Stephen, and it could well be that the seeds of uncertainty were sown by that incident. Often vehement protestation covers a deeper uncertainty. Stephen's witness must have been impressive, and even the hard-line Paul must have been struck by the reality of his faith.

By the time he undertook the journey to Damascus Paul's mind was in a turmoil; on the one hand he longed to cling to the custom and forms of his Pharisaic upbringing and training, and yet on the other he knew himself challenged by this new phenomenon. Into this whirlpool of emotions the Lord spoke and brought Paul to himself. From confusion and inner turmoil Paul's life was transformed. He came into a relationship with Jesus and discovered a calm certainty and assurance which enabled him to preach with power.

A new direction

Certainly the dramatic encounter on the road to Damascus left Paul in no doubt as to who was in charge. Paul was led into Damascus to await his orders. These directions come through the ministry of Ananias. Ananias came to Paul, laid his hands on him, his sight was restored and he knew the power of the Spirit. Immediately he was released into a new ministry and went to preach the truth about Jesus.

Little more is heard of Paul in the Acts until chapter 13 (we do know from elsewhere in the New Testament that he retreated for a time of study and meditation, preparing for his new life and public ministry). Later the Lord's call to Paul is confirmed: 'While they were serving the Lord and fasting, the Holy Spirit said to them, "Set apart for me Barnabas and Saul, to do the work to which I have called them"' (Acts 13:2). From this moment he began his life's work in earnest as the gospel travelled across the empire. Here was a man with a purpose given to him by the power of God's Spirit.

Ruled by the love of Christ

To be passionate or enthusiastic is not always popular in our present generation. It is thought much more important to be cool, level-headed, calm. Paul, following his meeting with the risen Lord Jesus, became passionate about the gospel. He immediately began to preach the good news that he had experienced. The rest of the book of Acts shows that he was a man compelled to bring the good news of Jesus to others. All of his letters, some of them the earliest written parts of the New Testament, echo with his passion for the gospel. We can note some examples:

◇ His commitment to Christ: 'For what is life? To me, it is Christ. Death then, will bring more' (Philippians 1:21).

◇ His passion for the truth of the gospel: 'Freedom is what we have—Christ has set us free! Stand, then, as free people, and do not allow yourselves to become slaves again' (Galatians 5:1).

◇ His desire to see others come to faith: 'Here we are, then, speaking for Christ, as though God himself were making his appeal through us. We plead on Christ's behalf: let God change you from enemies into his friends!' (2 Corinthians 5:20).

◇ His understanding of the centrality of the cross: 'For while I was with you, I made up my mind to forget everything except Jesus Christ and especially his death on the cross' (1 Corinthians 2:2).

All these speak of a man who had been moved by God's Holy Spirit and given a passionate desire to live under Christ's authority and to proclaim his good news.

Experiencing the power

Three days after his startling meeting with the risen Lord Jesus, Paul was met by Ananias who prayed with and for him, and laid hands on him. Paul received his sight back and also received the gift of the Holy Spirit. From that moment he realized that his life was not his own, nor was his life self-motivated. He recognized the rest of his life would be lived out in the power of the Holy Spirit who gave him the life of Jesus. In Galatians he wrote: 'I have been put to death with Christ on his cross, so that it is no longer I who live, but it is Christ who lives in me. This life that I live now, I live by faith in the Son of God, who loved me and gave his life for me' (Galatians 2:19–20).

And again: 'Let the Spirit direct your lives, and you will not satisfy the desires of the human nature' (Galatians 5:16).

And in verse 22 of that same chapter: 'The Spirit produces love, joy, peace, patience, kindness, goodness, faithfulness, humility and self-control.' The fruit of the Spirit gives the very life of Jesus to the believer. Paul, from the road to Damascus to his final trial in Rome, was a man who knew the Spirit empowering his ministry and filling his life.

Pause for thought

Reflect on today's studies and indeed all the studies of this week. Write in your diary the main features that have struck you and your reactions to them. How do you want the Lord to change your discipleship? Write your response in your diary.

Pause for reflection

In what ways do you know the peace, purpose, passion and power that the Holy Spirit wants to give you?

Pause for prayer

O thou who camest from above
The pure celestial fire to impart,
Kindle a flame of sacred love
On the mean altar of my heart.
Charles Wesley

Material for group study

For sharing

As individuals within the group, note down:

◇ the things that have been new to you and enlightened you

◇ the questions that have been raised.

Divide the group into pairs and give time for each pair to share their answers.

Let each pair write down on a piece of card the one insight they would like to bring to the whole group.

For learning

Put the pieces of card from the pairs on a table and discuss each issue raised in turn.

The leader could prepare similar cards with a key verse from each of the day's studies. Look at the issues and the key verses: are there any links or pointers?

For discussion and application

What are the points from the week's studies that the group would like to take to the whole church?

From these points write a brief fax which could be given or sent to the Church Council to help the whole church to discover the way forward in the power of the Spirit.

For prayer

List out the key issues and allow them to become pointers for prayer. Some of the group may like to pray aloud or the leader could mention each issue and then leave a time of silence finishing with the response:

Leader: *Come, Lord Jesus Christ*
All: *And fill us afresh with the power of your Holy Spirit.*

WEEK 4

THE HOLY SPIRIT IN THE LIFE OF THE INDIVIDUAL

There can be no doubt that God the Holy Spirit is back on the agenda of the Church. In one sense he has never been off that agenda, but in many ways until recent years his work has been either misunderstood or ignored.

There is a story about a Christian missionary sharing something of his faith with a Japanese friend. In response to the Christian's explanations the friend says that he understands something of God the Father, something of God the Son, but is very confused about the place of the 'Honourable Bird'.

Whilst in recent years many Christians have discovered the *significance* of the Holy Spirit in their individual discipleship there are many who would echo that sentiment and admit their confusion about the *person* of the Holy Spirit. Our studies this week help us to explore something of the person of the Spirit, in particular his work in the life of the individual disciple.

Over recent years great stress has rightly been laid on the corporate nature of the Church. No longer is discipleship seen in isolation. Christians are called to a relationship one with another within the body of Christ. However, it is important to realize that there can be no real fellowship between Christians unless there is first a relationship between the individual disciple and Jesus. It is that relationship which is the foundation upon which everything else is built. Until that is in place there can be no fellowship. Hence the need to look at the work of the Spirit in the individual.

To live a new life

Many Christians are aware of feelings of inadequacy and failure, and even the temptation to turn back from following Jesus. Many Christians experience a sense of defeat and seem to know little of the victory that is modelled in the New Testament. There is a key verse in helping us face this problem in Paul's first letter to the Thessalonians: 'He who calls you will do it, because he is faithful' (1 Thessalonians 5:24).

Paul called the Thessalonians to live a holy life in the peace of God. In their own strength that would have been an impossible task. God, though, does not lay heavy burdens upon us. He calls us to his service and then gives us his Spirit to help us.

Christians are called to live a holy life so that the power of heaven can be seen here on earth. We regularly pray 'Your kingdom come on earth as it is in heaven'. That will only be possible if we allow the Holy Spirit to fill us and empower us. The Holy Spirit is given so that the mind and image of Jesus might be formed in each one of us.

Power for all

Many have experienced the power of the Holy Spirit refreshing and reinvigorating their discipleship. They have discovered the fruit and gifts he gives and then experienced a new joy and intimacy in their relationship with Jesus Christ.

The power of the Holy Spirit is not given for our own personal satisfaction or gratification. We may experience a deepening joy and certainty within our hearts and lives but the Holy Spirit seeks to build us up so that we might be more effective and real in our fellowship one with another. The Spirit is given to individuals so that they might be a blessing to the many.

The Spirit's power is not for the chosen few or for those who happen to be in the right place at the right time. Quoting the prophet Joel on the day of Pentecost, Peter told his hearers that God's Spirit was being poured out on all who would receive him. God longs to pour out his Spirit in refreshment and renewal, day by day, on all those who look to him.

A gift to be received

The Holy Spirit is a gift of God's grace. He is not ours because we have merited his coming or have earned the right to receive him. He comes to those who recognize their need, admit their total dependence upon God and look for the powerful infilling of his Spirit.

It must be with an attitude of humility that we approach this week's studies and dare to ask the Lord to fill us afresh, or for the first time, with his Holy Spirit.

Day 1

The Holy Spirit and new birth

John 3:1–13

'I am telling you the truth,' replied Jesus. 'No one can enter the Kingdom of God without being born of water and the Spirit. A person is born physically of human parents, but is born spiritually of the Spirit. Do not be surprised because I tell you that you must all be born again. The wind blows wherever it wishes; you hear the sound it makes, but you do not know where it comes from or where it is going. It is like that with everyone who is born of the Spirit.' (vv. 5–8)

Some weeks after coming to faith, a friend of mine talked about his new-found relationship with Jesus Christ. He said that before he became a Christian it was as though he had been living in an egg, but now he had broken out. He paused and then added, 'It is just as though I have a new life,' and then as an afterthought said, 'Is it all right to say that?' I assured him that it was more than 'all right'. The experience that he described simply echoed the promise of Jesus.

New birth—new life

Sadly the phrase 'born again' has become one of abuse. This is mainly because of the way it is used by some people, particularly in the United States. But it is wrong to miss the truth because of a travesty of that truth. Jesus challenged Nicodemus to look beyond the formal structures of religion and to recognize that God alone could bring reality and power by the renewing of a person's spiritual life.

Jesus took Nicodemus to the heart of the 'spiritual' matter. As a Pharisee, Nicodemus would have been a student of the Law and followed the Pharisaic teachings. The Pharisees taught that if all Israel kept all the 614 precepts of the Law for one day, God's promised kingdom would come. Jesus gently helped this seeker after truth to realize that the issue was far deeper than just encouraging everyone to keep the Law!

By their nature, human beings are unable to keep the demands of the holy God. That impossibility was highlighted by Jeremiah who longed for people to be given a new heart of obedience. Jesus said that men and women need to have this spiritual dimension in their lives more vitally—literally brought again to life. The consequence of the Fall and the coming of sin into the world was that the relationship humankind had with God was broken. Our ability to relate to a spiritual being died. Only as our spiritual being is brought to life again by the power of the Holy Spirit can there be any prospect of renewed relationship. In the words of Jesus, we need to be 'born again'.

This 'new birth' is a gift of the Spirit and of God's grace. Jesus made clear to Nicodemus that, like the wind, the Spirit blows where he wills. It is not that we approach and use the Spirit but rather that he approaches and uses us. This speaks not only of God's sovereign power, but also of his will. Nicodemus, as an orthodox Pharisee, had thought that God could be 'found' and brought into the affairs of men and women simply by keeping rigidly to the Law. Jesus made it clear that the Spirit moves as the power of God to bring new life, under God's authority and sovereignty. Men and women cannot find God and bring him to earth. Of his sovereign will he has decided to reveal himself. As the Son came from heaven to reveal God's nature and purpose, so the Holy Spirit comes from the very heart of God to show us what he is like and to enable us to respond to our Creator.

Further reading

2 Corinthians 5:14–19; 1 Peter 1:1–14

Pause for thought

Take time to be still. As you begin a new week of study ask the Lord to speak to you afresh. In your diary write down the things that have struck you in today's readings.

Pause for reflection

God speaks to us of the things of heaven here on earth. What is your response to the truth that he longs to be the sovereign Lord in your life?

Have you experienced the new birth which the Spirit comes to bring? (If you think the answer to this question is 'no', perhaps you would like to use the prayer at the end of today's study. It might also be helpful to talk with a trusted Christian friend or leader.)

Pause for prayer

Lord, thank you
that your Spirit enables me to be born again
and that through Jesus Christ
I can know the promises of heaven.

A prayer for those who want to commit themselves to Jesus Christ for the first time or renew that commitment:

Lord Jesus Christ,
please forgive me for the times
I have refused your love and ignored your word.

I believe that you came to die that I might be forgiven.
And rose again so that I might have new life.

Please send your Holy Spirit
so that I can be born again,
and love and serve you
as the person you want me to be.
Amen.

If you have prayed this prayer it would be a good idea to tell a trusted Christian friend or your minister, who will be able to help you as you grow in your Christian faith and discipleship.

Day 2

The Holy Spirit and God's children

Romans 8:14–17

> *Those who are led by God's Spirit are God's children. For the Spirit that God has given you does not make you slaves and cause you to be afraid; instead, the Spirit makes you God's children, and by the Spirit's power we cry out to God, 'Father! my Father!'* **(vv. 14–15)**

What does it mean to have been 'born again'? What are the signs of new birth? How could and should the individual life change? This passage from Romans 8 shows us the relationship to God which the Spirit enables us to have. We are 'born again' to become the sons and daughters of God.

The word which Paul uses for 'Father' is the Aramaic word *Abba*. This, of course, echoes the words used by Jesus in the garden of Gethsemane, '*Abba*, Father! All things are possible for you. Take this cup of suffering away from me.'

At the point of intense struggle and inner conflict Jesus held onto God as his Father. The word *Abba* was an intimate term of endearment used by a Hebrew boy of his father—akin to the modern 'Daddy'. The close relationship which Jesus enjoyed with God is shared with the disciples by the power of the Holy Spirit.

Note how Paul uses the language of adoption. Christians are accepted into God's family; their status has become equal with that of the natural Son, Jesus. This picture of adoption is especially powerful for my own family. We have two natural children and an adopted daughter. Since Chloe became ours by adoption all three now share the same status, the same privileges and obligations. As parents we view each one as equal. This personal experience has brought alive in a most marvellous way what God has achieved through the cross of Christ. Those who trust in Jesus know the power of the Spirit confirming their adopted status and affirming that they are children of God.

Not slaves of fear

Before a person comes to Christ they are a slave to sin. Not everyone will recognize this condition, but nevertheless it is a fact. Without Christ everyone is in bondage to the power of sin, and to the ultimate consequence of sin which is death. Christ's death broke that enslaving power of sin. The Holy Spirit comes into the new-found freedom to take away the fear of death and to replace it with a living hope. The kingdom which Jesus preached becomes a reality in the heart of the believer; the prisoner is set free and the captive released.

Sharing the blessings

The New Testament shows us that this present age is not the sum total of God's plans. The secular approach always stresses the immediacy of need and that riches and status are to be gained in this present age. The Holy Spirit comes to assure God's children that their real hope is in heaven, and that is where they will discover their true inheritance. Just as we have to wait for a family inheritance, so we wait for the Lord's return in order to enter into the blessings he has stored up for us.

Because of Jesus' faithful obedience he has fulfilled the Father's will and won the right to enter heaven itself. The way of faith shown to Abraham has been fulfilled in Jesus and he has received all God's promises. Those who are 'in Christ', those who believe in him, share in the glory he has won.

Sharing Christ's sufferings and his glory

The status of being a child of God brings with it privileges and obligations. One of our responsibilities in this present age is to be willing to share in the suffering of our Lord Jesus. Jesus encouraged his disciples to take up the cross every day to follow him. Those who are really seeking to be sons and daughters of the living God will want to share in his work here on earth, and inevitably that will sometimes lead to suffering. It is because we hold the hope of glory before us that we have the courage to walk the way of suffering, the way of the cross here on earth.

Further reading

Galatians 4:4–7; Ephesians 1:5

Pause for thought

In your diary list what it means for you to be a child of God.

Pause for reflection

From the list you have put in your diary do you feel you have discovered the full implications of being a child of God?

What are the privileges and obligations which come with being a child of God?

Pause for prayer

Abba Father let me be
Yours and yours alone

Day 3

The Holy Spirit: power for new life

Romans 8:1–13

> *Those who live as their human nature tells them to, have their minds controlled by what human nature wants. Those who live as the Spirit tells them to, have their minds controlled by what the Spirit wants. To be controlled by human nature results in death; to be controlled by the Spirit results in life and peace.* (vv. 5–6)

Whilst the cross of Christ has won the ultimate victory over evil, sin and death, it is obvious that the battle against the power of Satan is still being waged. It is important for Christians to recognize that this struggle will continue until Christ returns and the power of the cross is fully seen. As Christians await the return of Christ they are called to live in the 'overlap period' as the kingdom of God breaks into the kingdom of darkness and seeks to set free all that Satan has bound and spoiled.

The human battlefield

The casualties of this continuing battle are all around us in broken lives and situations. Christians, seeking to live the new life of Jesus, frequently find themselves defeated by the power of the 'old' human nature.

The intensity of this inner struggle is at the heart of Paul's thinking at the end of Romans 7. He describes accurately the inner conflict experienced by us all. It is as we know the holiness and sovereignty of God in a new way that we become aware of our own weakness and failure. Chapter 7 ends with the heartfelt cry: 'What an unhappy man I am! Who will rescue me from this body that is taking me to death?' This cry of despair is immediately followed by the cry of victory: 'Thanks be to God, who does this through our Lord Jesus Christ!'

Victory won

How then is this victory given to us through Jesus Christ? In Romans 6, Paul explains that the power of sin and death has been defeated by the cross of Christ. It is by and through the cross that we can enter into a new relationship with God. However, having been given this new relationship, the power to continue in that relationship is a vital necessity. This power to live the new life is the subject of Romans 8. It is of course the power of the Holy Spirit.

In Romans 8, Paul shows us that there is no division between the person of Christ and the person of the Spirit. As a person turns to Christ and acknowledges and accepts his sacrifice on the cross, that person receives all the potential and power of the Holy Spirit—the gift of the risen Christ. Paul declares with confidence that the Spirit has set him free from the law of sin and death and then goes on to explain how the Spirit works in an individual's life.

Life in the Spirit

First, and very simply, the Holy Spirit helps the Christian to live according to the Spirit and not according to the 'old' human nature (v. 4). To live in such a way means that the Christian mind becomes controlled by what the Holy Spirit wants. Paul is concerned for the renewing of the Christian mind. He sees the mind as the controlling element within an individual's life. What conditions and controls the mind will condition, determine and control the whole life. It is crucial that the motivating power within our minds is that of the Holy Spirit.

Secondly, Paul goes on to describe the result of being empowered and renewed by the Spirit. In verse 6 he promises that to know the Spirit is to experience life and peace. The Holy Spirit brings to our everyday experience a taste of the abundant life which Jesus promised. Many people live an existence; the Spirit promises and brings life in all its fulness. This fulness is marked by the peace of God. Such peace does not mean the absence of conflict, nor does it remove the Christian from the difficult complexities of life. It is the assurance of peace with God and is a peace which stays with us in all circumstances.

Thirdly, Paul writes about the promise of eternity. The power which raised Jesus is the same power which gives us the promise and certainty of eternal life after death.

The consequences of living according to our human nature are almost too dire to contemplate. They are a continuing enmity with God and the taste of death in the present life and for eternity. It is this stark fact which encourages Paul to exhort his readers to open themselves to the gift of the Spirit and to live the life which he makes possible.

Paul takes up the same theme in Galatians 5. In verse 16 he declares: 'What I say is this: let the Spirit direct your lives, and you will not satisfy the desires of the human nature.' He shows the contradiction of the person claiming to be a Christian, but not demonstrating new life in discipleship. This leads him on to describe the fruit of the Spirit. This is the subject for tomorrow's study.

Further reading

Romans 7:18–25; Galatians 5:16

Pause for thought

In the silence allow God's Holy Spirit to show you those things in your life which are still formed by the old human nature and not by his power. Fill in your diary for the day.

Pause for reflection

In what ways do you allow the old human nature to defeat you? Where in your own experience do you recognize the struggle Paul speaks about?

Think of ways in which you can reorder your life to give God time to fill you afresh with his Holy Spirit.

Pause for prayer

Lord Jesus,
come to me afresh with the power of your Holy Spirit,
so fill me with that Spirit that
my mind is renewed
my life redirected
and I taste the power of heaven.
Amen.

Day 4

The Holy Spirit: the power of transformation

Galatians 5:16–26

> *But the Spirit produces love, joy, peace, patience, kindness, goodness, faithfulness, humility, and self-control. There is no law against such things as these. And those who belong to Christ Jesus have put to death their human nature with all its passions and desires. The Spirit has given us life; he must also control our lives. We must not be proud or irritate one another or be jealous of one another.* (vv. 22–26)

In his letter to the Galatians, Paul is defending the gospel against those who were trying to mislead many of the early Christians. He argues that people are not put right with God by what they do, but rather by putting their trust in what he has done for them through the cross. The Galatians had been troubled by those who claimed that the Law was still a necessity for salvation. Paul challenges this by stating that to revert to the Law means returning to slavery and foregoing the freedom won by Christ. It was this freedom that was a point of contention, because those who wanted to return to the Law claimed that Christian freedom was a licence for immorality.

Old life—new life

This is the context in which we turn to the second part of Galatians 5. Paul is eager to show that far from leading to immorality, a Christian lifestyle, empowered by the Holy Spirit, is meant to reflect the very qualities of Jesus. Today's study shows that the Holy Spirit must be present for the new life in Christ to be continued and lived out. The relationship between the believer and Jesus changes the life of the disciple. The relationship between the believer and the Holy Spirit produces outward signs which can be seen in the Christian fellowship and the wider world.

Before turning to the nine qualities of the fruit of the Spirit, Paul contrasts the life lived in the Spirit with that lived under the control of the 'old' human nature. If his opponents had been right, then living according to the Law would have manifested itself in outward quality of life. Paul, however, catalogues the signs of life lived according to the 'old' human nature—immorality, practice of idolatry, occult involvement and so on—which brings disunity, disorder and a sense of brokenness. These are signs of life lived without the invading and transforming power of the Holy Spirit. This gives the lie to his opponents' argument. Keeping outward religious formalities and seeking to keep the Law can never transform human nature.

Fruit of the Spirit

From this rather depressing picture Paul turns to the life lived in the Holy Spirit. For Paul, life in the power of the Spirit is to be a continuing daily experience. The Good News Bible translates verse 16 as 'let the Spirit direct your lives', but a closer translation of the Greek would be 'continually walking in the Spirit'. Discipleship is a daily journeying in the sphere and power of God's Holy Spirit. You might ask how a life lived in the sphere of the Spirit can be recognized. Well, just as we can identify an apple tree by its apples, or a pear tree by its pears, so we can recognize the fruit of the Spirit-filled and directed life. Paul lists the nine qualities of the fruit of the Spirit—love, joy, peace, patience, kindness, goodness, humility, faithfulness and self-control. We can link the qualities together in three sets of three.

Love, joy, peace

These are the three foundational qualities which the Holy Spirit brings into the life of the believer. Love is at the heart of God as he reaches out into his world and must be at the heart of every believer and the Christian community. It was the quality of this love, which so amazed the contemporary world of the early Church, and so gripped the early Christian community that they had to find a little-used Greek word, *agape*, to describe it. It is a love which reflects the self-giving nature of God himself and the love which must be the foundation of every Christian life. Closely linked with love are peace and joy.

As we saw yesterday, Christian peace is principally the peace which the believer has with God. Because he or she knows the forgiveness of God and the end of guilt and shame the disciple is released to live a new quality of life with others. No longer is there a concern either to hide the true self or enhance oneself. To know you are accepted sets you free to accept and love others. Similarly, Christian joy is not a superficial happiness but rather the deep-seated assurance of the promise of heaven and of the Lord's presence. Such joy brings release so that life can be lived with a willingness to forgive others and put others first.

These are the foundational qualities of the fruit of the Spirit. They are given by the Holy Spirit, they can never be achieved by our own human effort.

Patience, kindness, goodness

These three qualities could be called qualities of attitude. Probably all of us know people who are a blessing to others because of the attitude they bring to life.

The word patience has overtones of tolerance and of being willing to cope with people and situations even when they are sorely trying. It means being willing to work at a relationship because there is a recognition that the other person is also created in the image of God.

Kindness comes from the Greek word *chrestotes*, and the common slave name 'Chrestos' came from that word. Its origin helps the understanding of the word. It is a kindness which is willing to serve others and to give beyond the call of duty. Similarly goodness in its original meaning had the overtone of generosity of spirit. These three qualities are to mark the attitude of the Christian to those around him or her.

Faithfulness, humility, self-control

These three qualities of relationship speak for themselves. Faithfulness brings with it a sense of fidelity and loyalty in relationships and humility militates against an overbearing, arrogant attitude.

Finally, the Christian needs to display self-control no matter what the opposition or provocation.

The Holy Spirit is given to transform the life of the disciple. Where do we see the qualities of the fruits of the Spirit most fully? The answer is, of course, in Jesus. The Holy Spirit is given so that the characteristics of Jesus himself can be produced in the life of each believer. The word 'fruit' is itself significant. In his last night with his disciples Jesus spoke of the fruit that they should bear in their lives. The Holy Spirit makes that harvest possible.

For further reading

John 15:1–8

Pause for thought

In your diary write down the nine qualities of the fruit of the Spirit (Galatians 5:22–23). Take time to meditate upon them and measure your own life against them.

Pause for reflection

The Holy Spirit longs to produce his fruits in the life of every Christian. What are the areas of your own life at home, work and recreation where you are refusing to allow the Spirit to direct you?

In what ways is your life built on the foundations of love, joy and peace?

In what ways do others see patience, kindness and goodness in your attitude towards them?

In what way do you relate to others with faithfulness, humility and self-control?

Pause for prayer

Lord of the harvest,
produce the fruit of the harvest
of your Spirit in my life.
I pray this not for myself
but for your glory
and the blessing of others.
Amen.

Day 5

The Holy Spirit: assurance and guarantee

Ephesians 1:1–14

> *And you also became God's people when you heard the true message, the Good News that brought you salvation. You believed in Christ, and God put his stamp of ownership on you by giving you the Holy Spirit he had promised. The Spirit is the guarantee that we shall receive what God has promised his people, and this assures us that God will give complete freedom to those who are his. Let us praise his glory!* **(vv. 13–14)**

The opening verses of the letter to the Ephesians are like the opening bars of a great symphony. With great skill and passion Paul paints a picture of all that God has done through the Lord Jesus Christ. As the themes of the gospel come tumbling forth one after another Paul speaks of the universal significance of the cross, as well as its application to the individual. He shows that God has a purpose and plan which runs from eternity to eternity. The greatest marvel is that God in his love has called us into a relationship with him. We are called to share his blessings and to declare his glory.

The great vision

The marvellous vision in Ephesians is breathless in its scope and immense in its implications. These words were written to a small, hard-pressed church in the first century, wrestling with all the issues of its day.

Whilst we may live in very different circumstances and the issues facing us vary widely from those of the first century, nevertheless the same doubts and uncertainties come to our minds. Can these great words be taken as valid? And can promises about a future which God has planned be trusted? It is the Holy Spirit who is sent to our aid.

In verses 13–14 Paul gives two pictures of the work of the Holy Spirit—the Spirit as the seal or stamp of God's ownership and the Spirit as the guarantee of all God's promises.

The Spirit: stamp of God's ownership

Paul's readers would have been familiar with the purpose of a seal. The seal was the personal sign of an owner and was often used on letters and documents both to show their authenticity and to confirm that they had not been tampered with before they were received. We are familiar with this today. Paul sees the Holy Spirit as the stamp of God's ownership on a Christian's life. It is a mark of authenticity. The Spirit brings the assurance that we belong to God. How can I know that I am the Lord's? Because I experience his Holy Spirit and know the stamp or seal of his ownership upon me.

The Spirit as guarantee

In Paul's day, when an agreement was made between two parties, a part payment was made which guaranteed the full payment at the appropriate time. Paul goes on to link this idea of guarantee with that of redemption.

The term redemption comes from the slave markets of Paul's day. For a slave to be freed, a price had to be paid and this transaction was known as redemption. Paul uses the picture to show that we have been set free from slavery to sin and Jesus himself has paid the price and has redeemed us. However, in one sense, whilst we live in this world we are still subject to the power of sin. We look forward to that day when Jesus will set us free completely—when our redemption will be whole. The Holy Spirit is the guarantee that the transaction which began on the cross will be completed on the day of the Lord's coming.

It could be argued that to experience the Holy Spirit as a seal and guarantee is actually very subjective. It can only be something which we know within ourselves. How do we know that our personal experiences are a genuine mark of the Holy Spirit? With this in mind let us turn briefly from the letter to the Ephesians to the first letter of John.

Obedience, love and opposition

'Those who obey God's commands live in union with God and God lives in union with them. And because of the Spirit that God has given us we know that God lives in union with us' (1 John 3:24).

In this letter John is concerned to show that the Christian life must have a practical outworking. Like Paul, he recognizes that the new life to which the Christian is called is made possible by the power of the Holy Spirit. It is the Holy Spirit who both empowers us and assures us that we live in union with God. John gives three objective criteria to show that the assurance is real.

◇ First he says that those who live in union with God by the power of the Holy Spirit will have a growing inclination to be obedient to God's word. John is realistic enough to recognize that we will still fall and fail, but none the less there will be a gradual change in the life of the Christian to make him or her more Christ-like.

◇ Secondly, living in union with Christ will bring assurance of God's love. We will recognize that God took the initiative in loving us and that his love sets us free from all fear. As the Spirit reveals God's love, so we shall be released to love others. There must be a growing desire in the heart of the Christian to give love in every practical way.

◇ Thirdly, John recognizes that those who are led by the Spirit will inevitably face opposition in the world. This opposition is almost like an assurance in itself because it means that we are walking in the way of Jesus. This does not mean that we are deliberately to court opposition or persecution, but, if the Spirit is directing our hearts, we will find people speaking against those things that we hold true (1 John 3:13).

The Holy Spirit gives us the assurance that all God's promises to us are true and can be trusted. The great words of Paul at the beginning of Ephesians are not just flights of fancy but deep spiritual insights into the heart of God and of the nature of creation. As we allow the Holy Spirit to assure us of these promises then we can certainly say with Paul, 'let us praise God's glory'.

Further reading

2 Corinthians 1:21–22; 1 John 3:24; 4:13–18

Pause for thought

The Spirit is the stamp of God's ownership on the believer and the guarantee of all his promises. Do you know this experience and trust the guarantee? Write down your response in your diary.

Pause for reflection

In what ways do you know the Holy Spirit as a stamp of ownership?

Think of three promises about God's love and the gift of eternal life. Let the Holy Spirit guarantee to you that these promises can be trusted.

Do you know the Holy Spirit giving:

◇ transformation into the likeness of Jesus?

◇ an assurance of God's love?

◇ a struggle with the world?

Pause for prayer

God's love has been shed abroad in our hearts
by the Holy Spirit he has given us.
Father, please pour your Spirit into my heart
that I might both know and share your love.
Amen.

Day 6

The Holy Spirit and discipleship

1 Corinthians 2:10–16

But it was to us that God made known his secret by means of his Spirit. The Spirit searches everything, even the hidden depths of God's purposes. It is only the spirit within people that knows all about them; in the same way, only God's Spirit knows all about God. We have not received this world's spirit; instead, we have received the Spirit sent by God, so that we may know all that God has given us. **(vv. 10–12)**

Christian discipleship is an ongoing and daily working out of faith in Jesus Christ. Discipleship is to be in relationship with Jesus and that relationship has to affect every part of our lives. This doesn't happen all at once. We hold back various parts of our lives until we are ready to surrender them. The Holy Spirit longs to be involved in every part of our lives. Just as breathing brings life to every part of the body, so living in the Spirit brings spiritual well-being to every part of our discipleship.

The key passage and the further reading for this study give a taster to the many aspects of discipleship; some insights to the ways the Spirit enriches and empowers each individual's walk with God. In his word to the disciples on the last night of his life, Jesus promised that the Holy Spirit would come 'to lead them into all truth'. Amongst other things, the Spirit was to be the great illuminator bringing light to darkened minds. It is this thought that Paul pursues in his first letter to the Corinthians.

Understanding God

Discipleship begins with receiving the truth about God, and then needs to grow and continue. For many Christians, discipleship stagnates either because they do not realize that it is meant to be dynamic and moving forward or because they do not know how God wants them to develop. The Holy Spirit promotes our spiritual growth.

Guidance

Knowing God's will and his plan for our future can be notoriously difficult and guidance is the subject of many books. All we really need to know is that God wants us to learn his way and to have the strength to walk in it. Guidance is not a one-off phenomenon, it is to be an ongoing reality. In Colossians 1:9–10, Paul writes: 'We ask God to fill you with the knowledge of his will with all the wisdom and understanding that his Spirit gives. Then you will be able to live as the Lord wants and will always do what pleases him. Your lives will produce all kinds of good deeds, and you will grow in your knowledge of God.'

Our lives are to be living testimonies of God's power and presence. As we offer ourselves to his service and seek his will through meditation upon his word, through prayer and fellowship, and through circumstances, God promises that his Holy Spirit will make his way known to us; it remains for us to be faithful and obedient.

Prayer

Prayer is the key to this relationship. We shall only know the power of the Holy Spirit leading us into the heart of God, and that same power leading us from the heart of God into our walk of discipleship, if we are willing to give ourselves to him in prayer. Prayer was the focal point of the New Testament, both in the life of Jesus and in the early Church. However, today many people find the life of prayer very difficult and become dispirited very quickly.

It is at this point of struggle and discouragement that we need to discover again the power of God's Holy Spirit. Not only does the Spirit come to reveal God's heart to us and assure us of a relationship with him but he is also there to enrich and encourage us in our prayer life. In Romans 8:26–27, Paul writes: 'In the same way the Spirit also comes to help us, weak as we are. For we do not know how we ought to pray; the Spirit himself pleads with God for us in groans that words cannot express. And God, who sees into our hearts, knows what the thought of the Spirit is; because the Spirit pleads with God on behalf of his people and in accordance with his will.'

It is when we come to the end of our own resources that the Holy Spirit is there to empower us in our praying. It is at this point in our lives that we need to discover his influence afresh.

And the consequence is . . .

From this life of discipleship empowered by the Holy Spirit two consequences should flow.

First, we should discover a willingness to share the good news of the kingdom. It was as he was anointed by the Spirit that Jesus came preaching the good news. In 1 Thessalonians 1:5, Paul writes: 'For we brought the Good News to you, not with words only, but also with power and the Holy Spirit, and with complete conviction of its truth.'

Not all of us will be great public preachers but all disciples are called to be witnesses and, by the power of the Holy Spirit, to bring 'the conviction of the truth'. We live in a world that is hungry for truth and is willing to chase every fad and fancy. It is this spiritual vacuum that Christians should address in the power of the Spirit.

Secondly, 'All I want is to know Christ and to experience the power of his resurrection, to share in his sufferings and to become like him in his death, in the hope that I myself will be raised from death to life' (Philippians 3:10–11). Discipleship means meeting with the risen Lord and then being willing to let go of our lives for his sake and for the sake of the gospel, in the certain hope of the resurrection. We can not walk that way in our own strength, for it is far too costly. However, disciples empowered by the Spirit of Jesus should be willing to walk the way of Jesus and, as a result, will see honour and glory being given to his name, and blessing and new life brought to many people.

Further reading

Romans 12:1–2; Philippians 3:10; Colossians 1:9; 1 Thessalonians 1:5

Pause for thought

Reflect on your own discipleship with the Lord Jesus Christ. Where are you growing in discipleship and where do you need to be changed and strengthened? Complete your diary.

Pause for reflection

God longs to reveal more and more of himself to us through scripture and by the power of his Holy Spirit. In what ways do you seek and know the guidance of God through his Spirit? In what ways are you growing in the life of prayer?

Pause for prayer

Lord, come in the power of your Spirit.
Take me as I am
and make me into what you want me to be.
For Jesus' sake
Amen.

Day 7

A Spirit to be received

Acts 2:36–42

> *Peter said to them, 'Each one of you must turn away from your sins and be baptized in the name of Jesus Christ, so that your sins will be forgiven; and you will receive God's gift, the Holy Spirit.'* **(v. 38)**

In many life experiences there comes a point when you have to move from the theory to the practical. You might know all the theory about swimming but eventually the moment comes when you have to entrust yourself to the buoyancy of the water. Many children learn to ride a bike with an adult running behind holding them upright; in the end the supportive hand needs to be removed for the youngster to balance alone.

Up to this point we have been looking at the theory of the working of God the Holy Spirit. We must now ask him to fill our lives if we want his promises to become true in our own experience.

A troubled heart

As Peter preached his first sermon on the day of Pentecost, his hearers responded positively to his message. 'They were deeply troubled' and asked 'What shall we do?'

For many, the first experience of the Holy Spirit is when the Christian faith begins to come alive and make sense. Indeed, without the ministry of the Spirit it is impossible to come to a living faith. But, because the Church has often failed in its task to teach about God's Spirit, for many Christians the whole of his purpose and work remains a closed book.

As Christian discipleship develops there should be a growing hunger or yearning to know more of God's power and the fulness of his promises. Whether we have a troubled heart like Peter's listeners, whether we are confused about the person of the Spirit, or whether we are going through a period of dryness in our discipleship, God longs to pour his holy Spirit into our hearts and lives.

Whoever we are and whatever our circumstances, the Lord longs for us to move from the theoretical into an experience of his power at work within us.

Not just once

In his letter to the Ephesians Paul exhorts his readers to 'be filled with the Spirit' (5:18). The original Greek means 'go on being filled with the Spirit'.

As with so many aspects of discipleship, receiving God's Spirit should be an ongoing daily experience. Each day as I rise to greet the new morning, I need to ask God to fill me afresh with his Holy Spirit so that I might walk closely with him, shine in his light, and seize every opportunity to share his good news. Perhaps it has been a long while since you knew the joy of the Lord Jesus filling your heart and life. Begin again today by humbly asking the Lord to fill you.

It may be that sin has marred your relationship with the holy God. Let today be the day when the Lord deals with you, creates a pure heart within you and gives the gift of his Spirit.

A gift to be given

The whole of the New Testament is clear that all we have and are as disciples of the Lord Jesus is a gift of God's grace. Nothing we do can earn his blessing or favour; all is a gift from him. This is certainly true of the Holy Spirit. Peter tells the crowd that God wants to give the gift of his Spirit. This gift was not just for that occasion or that place. The gift is not limited by time or space. Whoever and wherever we are, God longs to pour this gift into our hearts. Whoever you are as you read today's studies, and whatever your circumstances, the Lord wants you to experience the gift of his Holy Spirit. It is a gift which goes on being offered until the end of time.

A gift to be received

As with all gifts, this gift of God has to be received. All of us will have received gifts which have been put to one side or even recycled and passed on to someone else. Equally, each of us has gifts which we received gladly, opened and still continually use and treasure. The only limitation placed upon the gift of the Holy Spirit is our openness and willingness to receive him. Today God offers his gift and longs for you to open yourselves to receive.

Seek, ask, receive

At the end of today's study notes there is a prayer you might like to use. As you seek the Holy Spirit, he may come quietly and gently like the descending dove; he may come dramatically and powerfully like the wind and the fire. Take time to be still and know that your heavenly Father will give the blessing of his Holy Spirit; for those who ask will receive.

Pause for thought

Take time to be quiet and reflect on your discipleship. Are you growing in your love for Jesus Christ? Have you come to a point where your faith and love need deepening? Record your thoughts in your diary.

Pause for reflection

The Holy Spirit longs for you to come to the point where you are ready to open yourself to his power, either afresh or for the first time. How do you respond to this truth?

If you think you need to know the power of the Holy Spirit in a new way, you might like to use the following prayer.

Pause for prayer

Lord Jesus Christ,
thank you that you long to pour out
the gift of your Holy Spirit
upon all who will receive him.
Please forgive me for the times
I have grieved your Holy Spirit,
or refused to allow him to rule in my life.
Please forgive me for the times
I have been afraid of your Spirit
and not trusted your love.

Today, I ask you to pour your Spirit into my life.
Help me to know your love in my life,
to experience your peace and joy,
and give me power boldly to proclaim your gospel.
Amen.

The Lord promises to give his Holy Spirit to those who ask him. He may come quietly and gently like a dove, or he may come with signs of dramatic power. If you have prayed this prayer it would be helpful to speak to a trusted Christian friend or to your minister. It may be that you would like to pray the prayer with that friend or minister.

Material for group study

For sharing

As individuals within the group, note down:

◇ the things that have been new to you and enlightened you

◇ the questions that have been raised.

Divide the group into pairs and give time for each pair to share their answers.

For learning

The leader gives out photographs of children and babies. Discuss the ways in which Christians are so often like babies and have failed to grow in discipleship. What are the hindrances to Christian growth and maturity and how can growth be encouraged?

Put out pieces of card with one aspect of the fruit of the Spirit on each. How can Christians be encouraged to allow the Spirit to fill their lives and reproduce his fruit? What difference would it make to the life of a congregation?

For discussion and application

How can points raised in the section above be brought to the whole church in a way which is helpful and constructive? How can we encourage each other to be filled with the Spirit?

For prayer

Take the nine qualities of the fruit of the Spirit. Let each person write a sentence about one of them. Individuals in the group or the group leader might like to read the sentences out in a time of shared prayer.

WEEK 5

THE HOLY SPIRIT IN THE LIFE OF THE CHURCH

This week we turn our attention to the Church and the place of the Holy Spirit within its life. Although the Church has been around since the day of Pentecost, there is much popular misunderstanding about its purpose. One of the most common claims, and yet one of the greatest delusions, is that you can be a Christian and not go to church. It is not surprising that this is the view of those outside the structure of the church, but even keen Christians can tend to see the Church as an optional extra and not an integral part of their discipleship. Church membership can become one amongst many options. The understanding of the early Church was very different and their expectations of the Holy Spirit must be a challenge to us all.

'Let the Church be the Church'

These words of the great theologian Emile Brunner ring as true today as they did when they were first spoken. Sadly, the Church is often paralysed by its own structures and plans and it fails to be what the Lord wants it to be. We can so easily be caught up with the immediacy of our own problems that the Holy Spirit is never allowed to set new horizons. The outward form can become so much more important than the inner reality, the Church becoming little more than a clanging gong or a noisy cymbal! This hollowness can affect the life of the Church at every level, from the national organization to the local congregation and even the community house group or fellowship meeting.

It is into this emptiness that the Spirit longs to flow, bringing his power for renewal and such a taste of the Lord's love and of heaven that Church life is transformed and the church does indeed become the Church.

Pictures of community

We may feel dissatisfied with our current experience of Church life and long for the Holy Spirit to flow and fill us afresh. But what is the Church for and how should its life be formed and structured? One fundamental principle becomes clear as we read Paul's letters. Primarily the Church is called to be the community of God's people.

All the pictures which Paul gives of the Church are community images. He speaks of the Church as a family, a nation, a people. These are obvious pictures of community, but there are other examples which may not be so obvious.

A body has its own integrity and wholeness but is nevertheless the community of its different parts, each working for the benefit of the other and of the whole. Similarly, buildings are the community of all the various parts which make up their whole structure—if one brick or concrete beam fails, the inherent strength of the building is weakened and there could even come a point where the building collapses. Each Christian is called to be part of the community of God's people, each individual interrelating with others in the Church, and all having an interdependence with each other to make the whole.

Making Jesus known

Paul shows us that as Christians are united together within the Church they become in their sum total the body of Jesus. If Jesus had remained on earth following the resurrection he would have been limited by space and time, now he dwells in his body, the Church. The task of the Church is to make Jesus known in all the fulness of his character and ministry. The body of Jesus is to share in the worship of Jesus, to bring the wholeness and healing of Jesus, and to proclaim the good news of his love and forgiveness to a lost and broken world.

Saying 'yes' to the Spirit

All too frequently, Christians in the Church say yes to the calling and to God's agenda but fail to recognize that God's work can only be fulfilled by God's power. Trying to fulfil God's longing without his power is like trying to driving a high-powered sports car without petrol to run the engine.

On the day of the ascension, the early Church said 'yes' to the Lord's commission, but it was only as they said 'yes' to his Holy Spirit on the day of Pentecost that they were able to go and proclaim the gospel and lead men and women to a living faith.

Day 1

The Spirit and the body of Jesus

Acts 9:1–9

'Who are you, Lord?' he asked. 'I am Jesus, whom you persecute,' the voice said. (v. 5)

It was probably at the moment of conversion that Paul began to understand the nature of the Church.

An important meeting

Paul had persecuted the early Christian Church, and his hatred for the followers of Christ had intensified after the death of Stephen. On his way to Damascus with the authority of the high priest to continue his violent pressure against the Church, Paul was met by the risen Lord Jesus Christ. The Lord's first words to him are significant: 'Why do you persecute me?' The persecution and physical violence was of course aimed at the individual Christians but, as they bore the pain inflicted by the authorities, Jesus too shared their suffering. There is evidence to suggest that it was probably from that moment that Paul began to realize that the Church was the body of Jesus here on earth—that his persecution of the followers of Christ was synonymous with persecuting Christ himself. Some years were to elapse before he worked out this thinking more fully, but certainly in many of his letters, particularly in his first letter to the Corinthians, he teaches that the Church is the body of Jesus. It is important to note that he does not say it is *like* a body. The phrase is not a convenient simile or picture language; Paul is saying something far more significant.

The body of Jesus

After the resurrection, although not limited by time, space and physical restrictions, it seems that Jesus only appeared to the disciples in one place and at one time. Following the ascension and his return to glory in heaven, Jesus kept his promise and poured his Holy Spirit upon the community of Christian believers. Paul teaches that, as well as bringing power and transforming lives, the Holy Spirit also brought that disparate group of believers together in fellowship and community as the Church. Furthermore, he claims that each gathering of local believers in a congregation became more than the sum of the believers. By the power of the Holy Spirit, Jesus resided amongst and within them and, by the power of the Holy Spirit, they became his body. It is as though the incarnation of God's Word, in the human body of Jesus during his earthly ministry, now continued in his heavenly reign as he dwelt in his body, the Church. In the Church, Jesus is still present here on earth and no longer limited by geographical location. Jesus is present wherever his Church is gathered.

Of course, the ministry of the Jesus through the Holy Spirit is not limited to the Church. He continues to be at work in the world in many and varied ways. But the Church has a significant role in continuing his work within the world, because it is an expression of his body. This truth shows why Paul was so concerned for the integrity and stability of the Church and spent so much of his ministry teaching, praying and longing for the Church to recognize its calling and to become more and more what it was meant to be. This need to rediscover the calling of the Church is no less important today and I hope the studies this week will enable local congregations to explore what the Holy Spirit wants them to become and longs to make them.

As we have already said, one of the biggest delusions about Christianity today is that a person can be a Christian and not go to church. Such a statement would be completely meaningless to our early Christian forbears. It is impossible to be a Christian and not be part of the Church. Commitment to Christ and rebirth in the power of the Holy Spirit mean that a person becomes part of his Church. To say that this is not so would be like saying that a baby is born, but has no need to be part of a family. Whatever the circumstances of birth, a blood relationship can never be denied. Christians, particularly in the West, where the privatization of the individual is paramount, need to work out what it really means to be part of Christ's body—that means the privileges as well as the responsibilities. In 1 Corinthians 12 Paul gives various insights into this.

Christ is a single body (v. 12). The body is called to be a unity. Each congregation is an expression of the body of Christ, as is the gathering of the wider universal Church. We have already seen that to be born again into Christ is to become part of his body. But Paul goes on to show that whilst there is one body there are great varieties within it. Every member is different, bringing different spiritual and natural gifts as well as strengths and weaknesses of character and personality.

Just as God wanted it (v. 18). Paul is concerned that the differences should not cause Christians to move apart from each other, but should allow the differences to enrich the whole. Just as in the human body, so in the body of Christ, each constituent part needs to work effectively for the good of the complete body. This spirit of interdependence also leads to a spirit of mutual care and encouragement (v. 26).

Someone has said that Christians are often like billiard balls which have hard exteriors and canon off each other. This is not what Jesus wants. He longs for the members of his body to be united and committed one to another.

One and the same Spirit (v. 11). In our own strength we have no real hope of becoming what the Lord of the Church wants. As in every aspect of our individual discipleship, it is the Spirit who enables and empowers. It is he who gives the gifts and binds the individual members into a community of love, mutual respect and true fellowship.

Sadly, this coming together of the body of Christ is not true of many congregations. There is still much individualism and privatization in discipleship. It was Paul's prayer in Galatians 4 that Christ's body should be formed amongst them. This must be our prayer for the congregation of which we are members, longing that in ever deeper ways we will indeed become the body of Jesus.

Further reading

1 Corinthians 12:1–26; Galatians 4:19–20

Pause for thought

Reflect for a moment on the life of the Church and your part within it. Are you willing to become an integral part of the body of Jesus? Write down your feelings and response in your diary.

Pause for reflection

What are the things which prevent you from playing a full part within the body of Jesus? Why do we so often resist the Holy Spirit's longing to make us into the body of Jesus?

Pause for prayer

Revive your Church, O Lord
And let your Power be shown
The gift and grace shall be ours
The glory yours alone!

A. Midlane © Jubilee Hymns

Day 2

The Spirit and the living temple

Ephesians 2:14–22

So then, you Gentiles are not foreigners or strangers any longer; you are now fellow-citizens with God's people and members of the family of God. You, too, are built upon the foundation laid by the apostles and prophets, the cornerstone being Christ Jesus himself. He is the one who holds the whole building together and makes it grow into a sacred temple dedicated to the Lord. In union with him you too are being built together with all the others into a place where God lives through his Spirit. **(vv. 19–22)**

To see the context for today's study let's briefly recap some of the insights from the first two weeks.

A quick recap

In the studies of the Old Testament it was seen that, throughout the history of Israel, God was seeking a dwelling place amongst men and women where he could reveal his glory and truth. The people of Israel became his chosen nation. During the wanderings in the wilderness and then during the early years of settlement in the Promised Land he was amongst them in the symbol of the tent of presence.

With the coming of King David and the extension of the kingdom there was a growing desire to build the temple as a symbol of God's dwelling. It fell to David's son, Solomon to construct this building and in 2 Chronicles 5:13–14 we read how the glory of the Lord came and rested on the building.

The centuries that followed saw apostasy and unfaithfulness. Through their disobedience the Jewish nation hid the glory of the Lord and the original intention of the temple was lost. It had always been the Lord's desire that, through his glory present in the temple, the nations of the earth would be drawn to him in worship and obedience. Through their disobedience the Jews thwarted that purpose and, when punishment came in the form of the exile, the temple was destroyed. Perhaps more significantly, the prophet Ezekiel saw the Lord's glory withdrawing from the temple.

The people of Israel never believed the glory returned to the temple that followed and it seemed the Lord was silent and heaven closed until the coming of Jesus. Jesus claimed to be the new temple, the dwelling place of God amongst men and women, and John was able to declare: 'We saw his glory, the glory which he received as the Father's only Son' (John 1:14). The Lord's glory had returned to the new temple.

The new temple

With the day of Pentecost came the birth of the Church. As we saw yesterday, Paul saw that the Church was the body of Jesus and that Jesus' earthly ministry was to be continued through his Church, by the power of his Holy Spirit. God was still to be present amongst us.

For Paul the implications of being the body of Jesus were many and varied. Here in Ephesians, he explores the responsibility of the Church being, with Jesus, the new dwelling place of God—the new temple.

Paul, in the first part of Ephesians 2, declares that all the old divisions between Jew and Gentile had been broken down by the cross of Christ. What failed to happen in the Old Testament had become a reality in the New. The Gentiles, partly through the Jews' disobedience, are now drawn to the living God—not only drawn to him but are part of his work. Ephesians 2:19 highlights this: 'So then you Gentiles are not foreigners or strangers any longer; you are now fellow-citizens with God's people and members of the family of God.' There is now only one people of God, Jew and Gentile drawn together through the death of Christ, but also sharing the one Spirit.

Towards the end of the passage, Paul develops his argument by introducing the picture of a building. It is as though each individual Christian, as well as being part of the body of Christ, is also a brick to be used in God's building site. Paul explains how the building is founded on the teaching of the apostles and prophets and that Jesus is the cornerstone which holds all of it together. The significance for today's study is Paul's understanding of the purpose of the building

It is a sacred temple where God can dwell in the power of his Spirit. The work, begun way back in the Old Testament, is moving towards its completion in the Christian Church. As the early Church allowed the Holy Spirit to move through it and rest within it, it became the dwelling place of God, the place where again his glory might be seen.

Becoming the temple

This understanding of the Church as the temple of the living God is not limited to the apostle Paul. Peter, in his first letter, takes up the same theme. Once again, the individual stones and building components are the lives of Christians and, again, Christ is the cornerstone upon which the whole is founded and finds its strength and integrity. However, Peter adds two further insights.

First, there is to be a submissiveness on the part of the disciple. Peter says 'Let yourselves be used in building the spiritual temple' (1 Peter 2:5). For all of us there needs to be a willingness to be placed where the Lord wants us. The raw materials cannot argue with the architect and the master builder. He knows what is best for each individual and for the whole and must be trusted.

Secondly, not only are we called to be the building but also the holy priests who serve there: 'Be used in building the spiritual temple, where you will serve as holy priests to offer spiritual and acceptable sacrifices to God through Jesus Christ' (1 Peter 2:5). The work of the priesthood in sacrificing for sin was done once and for all on the cross by Jesus. However, there is still a need to make God's glory known through the worship of his people. Christians are called to be priests, to bring men and women into the Lord's presence through the ministry of worship and of prayer. As the dwelling place of God in his world this continues to be our calling.

Further reading

2 Corinthians 3:18; 1 Peter 2:4–8

Pause for thought

Reflect on the privilege of being part of God's living temple. What does it really mean for today? After a period of quiet write down your response in your diary.

Pause for reflection

What are the things that prevent you from being a willing 'stone' in the Lord's temple? How can we help each other to allow the Holy Spirit to build the Lord's dwelling place among us?

Pause for prayer

Lord, forgive me
for the times I refuse to be part of your Church,
and forget all the privileges and responsibilities
that you have given to me.
Help me to be open to the power of your Spirit,
and to be a willing part of your spiritual temple.

Day 3

The Spirit and unity

Ephesians 4:1–6

Do your best to preserve the unity which the Spirit gives by means of the peace that binds you together. There is one body and one Spirit, just as there is one hope to which God has called you. (vv. 3–4)

It is a striking fact that during his last evening with his disciples Jesus spent so much time praying for them and for those who would come after them. Most people in his situation would have had their minds dominated by the coming struggle and would have been looking for support and encouragement. Jesus spent time in teaching. Then he prayed for his disciples and for us, as recorded in John 17.

One of the main thrusts of that prayer is that his followers might be one. This concern for unity was not simply for the well-being of Christians, but because such unity would reflect the very nature of the Godhead and would bring an unbelieving world to an acceptance of his mission. Unity is not an optional extra. Unity is to be at the very heart of the Christian Church. It is a prerequisite if the Church is really to be an instrument for God's ministry and mission.

The longing for unity

This theme of unity is a driving force in the teaching and writing of Paul. He, of all the early Christian leaders, knew what it was to be isolationist and cut off from his fellow human beings. Before his conversion, as a strict Pharisee, he would have shunned contact with any who were thought ritually unclean and would have had little time for the Gentiles or those considered outside God's grace. Following his conversion experience on the road to Damascus, Paul's spiritual eyes were opened by the Holy Spirit. He began to see things in a new way. It was a sense of God's desire for unity that burned within him and made him stand against any issue which would bring about disunity within the life of the Church. There are six areas worthy of consideration.

Unity—a gift of the Spirit. Paul is convinced that unity is a gift of the Spirit. This gift of unity is primarily to the Church, but eventually will come to the whole created order (see Ephesians 1:10; Colossians 1:16). As a gift of God this unity is non-negotiable. It is God's desire that the Church should receive and live in that unity which the Spirit gives. To reject that gift is to respond in disobedience to the giver.

Unity—reflecting the nature of God. The Spirit longs to bring unity to the Church, for the Church will then reflect on earth what is at the heart of heaven. Taking up the same theme as Jesus, Paul recognized that at the heart of the whole of creation lies the unity of the Godhead. To deny the gift of unity is to deny the very nature of God himself and that cannot be an option for a disciple who is wanting to walk in the Lord's way.

Unity—the reversing of disunity. Under the hand of God and by the power of his Holy Spirit, varied and disparate groups are taken and moulded into one. The core group of the apostles is striking in its variety—from brash fisherman to repentant tax-gatherer. The Holy Spirit took them and moulded them into the foundational unit of the early Church.

However, the Holy Spirit worked far beyond the scope of that original band. On the day of Pentecost, a multi-faceted and varied crowd suddenly heard in their own native languages the message of what God had done. The disunity of the tower of Babel was reversed in the unity of understanding on the day of Pentecost. As the Church spread and grew, the old enemies, the Samaritans and the hated Roman Gentiles, were all brought within the sphere of the Church by the unity given by the Spirit. The reality of unity in heaven became a living, practical reality on earth as disunited threads and strands were woven into a beautiful pattern.

Concern for unity. The early Church leaders realized that they needed to work hard to maintain unity and to give the Spirit room to move and complete his work. Soon after the birth of the Church, disunity was threatened by the squabble between the Jewish and Greek widows. The apostles recognized this challenge to unity and quickly moved to contain it. Men, filled with the Holy Spirit, were appointed to deal with this practical problem. However, much more was at stake than the practical issue of the amount of the daily distribution. Unity was threatened and it required Spirit-filled leadership to re-establish and maintain the integrity of the Church (Acts 6:1–7).

On a wider scale, as the Church spread and as Samaritans and Gentiles were brought into the new life of the Spirit, the leadership saw the need to keep doors of communication open. Peter and John quickly visited the Samaritan Church; Peter returned to Jerusalem after Cornelius received the Spirit, to explain the events; Paul, the apostle to the Gentiles, sought to keep in touch with the Church leadership in Jerusalem. Each in turn recognized that these momentous events could have threatened the unity of the Church and they needed to work with the Holy Spirit to maintain it.

Unity and Christian fellowship. In his final prayer at the end of 2 Corinthians, Paul speaks of fellowship in the Spirit. This is the great expression of unity within the Church. Fellowship is not simply a comfortable gathering of the like-minded, it is to be a practical outworking of Christian love and concern amongst those who hold in common the Lordship of Jesus Christ. The Spirit brings the gift of unity in order that we might enjoy fellowship with the risen Christ and with one another.

Maintaining the unity of the Spirit. Every Christian needs to ensure unity is maintained. Frequently that will mean counting others better than ourselves, walking the way of service, being willing to forgive and being ready to receive forgiveness. These are not natural human attributes. At all points it is vital to seek the power of the Holy Spirit.

Further reading
John 17:20–23; 2 Corinthians 13:14

Pause for thought
The Holy Spirit longs to bring unity to the people of God. Are there things in your life which prevent that unity being complete? Write down your response in your diary and turn your words into a prayer.

Pause for reflection
How often do you reflect on the unity which is at the heart of God the Father, Son and Holy Spirit? What part can you play in allowing their unity to become a model for the Church? Why do we find it so hard to preserve the unity of the body which is the Church, and how can we distinguish between issues of pride and principle?

Pause for prayer
'How wonderful it is, how pleasant,
for God's people to live together in harmony!' (Psalm 133:1).

Father, I know that this is your longing for your people.
Please forgive my part in the breaking of the body of Jesus,
and empower me with your Holy Spirit,
that I might be an instrument for unity.
In Jesus' name.
Amen.

Day 4

The Spirit and his gifts (1)

1 Corinthians 12:7–11, 27–31

The Spirit's presence is shown in some way in each person for the good of all. The Spirit gives one person a message full of wisdom, while to another person the same Spirit gives a message full of knowledge. One and the same Spirit gives faith to one person, while to another person he gives the power to heal. The Spirit gives one person the power to work miracles; to another, the gift of speaking God's message; and to yet another, the ability to tell the difference between gifts that come from the Spirit and those that do not. To one person he gives the ability to speak in strange tongues, and to another he gives the ability to explain what is said. But it is one and the same Spirit who does all this; as he wishes, he gives a different gift to each person. (vv. 7–11)

Today and tomorrow our studies look at the issue of spiritual gifts and their place and importance within the body of Christ, the Church. Much has been said and written about the gifts of the Spirit in recent years and some have found the teaching very hard to accept. Others have found the idea of shared ministry around the gifts not only helpful but liberating. I hope these next two days will open up the subject in a way which will be positive and constructive.

Setting the scene

Before we look at the readings from 1 Corinthians in detail, it is important to set them in context. Paul had been involved in the founding of the church at Corinth, but his letter shows that as the church developed there had been all kinds of stress, division and even immorality within it. One of the foremost issues had been a spirit of arrogance and pride within the membership. This pride had shown itself in attachment to various church leaders in a way which was bringing division to the heart of the church (1 Corinthians 1:12).

A further divisive issue was over the matter of spiritual gifts. It would appear that members of the church were using the gifts to enhance their own reputation and the gift was becoming more important than the giver. Furthermore, some gifts, such as speaking in tongues and prophecy, were held to be of greater value than some of the more practical gifts like administration and helping. Far from the Spirit bringing unity, there was disorder, jealousy and division.

It would also seem from what Paul says that the gifts were all being used at the same time in church meetings. This was particularly true of the gift of tongues. It would seem that some within the Corinthian church had exalted this particular gift above all others, and church meetings were simply becoming a confused babble as members used the gift in a very self-centred way. In this chapter and in 1 Corinthians 14, Paul clearly says that not all will speak in tongues, that tongues are useful for private edification (1 Corinthians 14:4) but if the gift is used within the context of public church worship then there must be an interpretation (1 Corinthians 14:27–28).

Paul lays down principles which are as relevant for the Church today as they were for the church in Corinth.

Gifted by the Holy Spirit

1 Corinthians 12 makes clear that the body of Christ, the Church, is to receive gifts from the Holy Spirit. The various gifts are listed in verses 8–11 and again in verses 27–28. This is not an exhaustive list—other gifts can be found in Ephesians 4 and Romans 12. (A list of gifts of the Holy Spirit mentioned in the Bible is set out in Appendix I on page 186.)

The purpose of spiritual gifts is to equip fully the body of Jesus. Just as the Holy Spirit produces fruit in the life of the believer in order that the character of Jesus can be seen, so the Spirit gives gifts to the Church so that the full ministry of Jesus can be exercised and experienced.

All for one and one for all

All who are disciples, and therefore members of the body, will receive a gift from the Holy Spirit which they are to bring for the good of the body. It is important to note that this gifting is not to build the status of the recipient, but is to be exercised in order that the Church might grow and become what the Lord wants it to be. The gifts are for each individual member, but for the blessing of all. It seems to be a New Testament principle that whilst an individual might receive a gift, the discernment of that gift had to be affirmed by the wider Church and thus properly authorized.

Paul is eager to stress that no gift is more important than another—all are equally necessary for the well-being of the body. Just as in the human physical body there is interdependence between the different parts, so it is with the spiritual body of Christ. None can be magnified above the others. This runs contrary to human nature. In the world of Corinth and in our own culture, status is the name of the game. We need to know where we stand in the pecking order. The Corinthians were exalting the more dramatic gifts and giving them a higher status. Paul's warning must be heeded by the Church today. There is no order of status within the Church. Each gift must be received and used within the spirit of service and certainly no gift must be counted more important than another. Mutual concern and love must be at the heart of the exercising of the gifts.

A spiritual health warning

In a further warning Paul deals with the distribution of the gifts. Reading between the lines of the letter, it would appear that some Corinthians were grasping at the gifts or claiming to be more endowed than others. Paul stresses that all are members of the body, but not all have all the gifts. Verses 29–30 are actually shown in the Greek as a series of questions. In the Greek it is possible to ask a question in such a way as to indicate that you are expecting the answer 'no'. Such is the construction here. By using this particular form of sentence, Paul stresses that all the gifts would not reside in one person. They are shared and given by the Lord's initiative and by the Spirit's power throughout the congregation.

This must be our expectation today. All too frequently it is assumed that spiritual gifts are simply 'sanctified' natural talents. Whilst it may be true that our God-given personalities and abilities might be further enriched by the Holy Spirit after we have become Christians, it is also true to say that the Holy Spirit can give new and specific gifts which must be received, discerned and used in the context of the Church. For example, an individual may believe that he or she has received the gift of healing—equally the church leadership may be led to recognize a gift in an individual who has not identified it themselves. In either case this initial recognition needs to be tested by prayer and discernment and affirmed, and then validated for use by and in the wider Church. Such a process should be applied to all the gifts. The same Lord longs to equip his body of the Church with all the gifts of the Spirit, so that his ministry can grow and move forward. They are distributed amongst the many and they are then moulded by the Holy Spirit into a beautiful unity.

Love is the name of the game

From 1 Corinthians 12 Paul moves to 1 Corinthians 13 the great passage of love. The greatest gift the Spirit brings to the heart of the disciple and the community of God's people is the gift of Love. In Romans 5:5 Paul says: 'God has poured out his love into our hearts by means of the Holy Spirit, who is God's gift to us.' That love is the love of Christ which moulds and welds the different members together.

To describe this Christian love, the Church used the word *agape*, a love which reflected God's willingness to give of himself. Try reading the verses of chapter 13 three times. First, use the word 'love'. Then replace the word 'love' with the word 'Jesus'. Finally, replace the word 'Jesus' with your own Christian name. The effect can be challenging and compelling.

It is vital that the exercise of the gifts of the Spirit is deeply rooted and grounded in the love of Christ. The gifts replicate his ministry. That can only be done with any integrity if they are used in the context of the love of Jesus, shining through each believer and dwelling at the heart of his Church.

Further reading

1 Corinthians 13

Pause for thought

Do you know the gift which the Holy Spirit has given you? If you are not sure, does the thought of receiving a gift fill you with anticipation or alarm? Take time for honest reflection before completing your diary.

Pause for reflection

How much do you see the gifts of the Holy Spirit in your local church? Do you believe they should be sought and exercised? Why are we so often afraid of the gifts God wants to give? How can you play your part in ensuring they are used in love?

Pause for prayer

Lord Jesus Christ,
as you pour out your Holy Spirit upon the Church,
help us to recognize all the gifts you are giving,
and teach us to use the gifts with humility as well as love.
For the glory of your name
Amen.

Day 5

The Spirit and his gifts (2)

Ephesians 4:7–16

He did this to prepare all God's people for the work of Christian service, in order to build up the body of Christ. And so we shall all come together to that oneness in our faith and in our knowledge of the Son of God; we shall become mature people, reaching to the very height of Christ's full stature. **(vv. 12–13)**

We have seen that God wants his Church to accept the gifts of the Holy Spirit humbly and then use them correctly. Properly used, the gifts can release Church members into a new life of service. Instead of being a chore, ministry can become an exciting adventure in faith as individuals discover the gifts the Lord has given them and then use those gifts for the good of the whole Church.

In today's reading Paul lays down some further principles about the use of the gifts. These principles are as relevant for the Church today as they were for the church in Ephesus.

Caught by the Lord

Probably all of us can cite horror stories about the misuse of the gifts of the Holy Spirit. Over the years there has been unhelpful and even false teaching about the gifts, and certainly in some instances, gifts have been used in an arrogant and high-handed manner. It is inevitable that if we experience gifts being misused, or have actually been hurt by their misuse, then we recoil from them. However, the misuse of gifts does not deny their blessing and value when they are used properly. We need to rediscover the teaching in the New Testament and then ensure that our Church leadership allows the use of the gifts according to biblical principles.

A fundamental principle is that the gifts must be used with a deep sense of humility. It is only when people become proud and self-important because they have a particular gift that disruption and division follow. Paul gives two reasons why we should remain humble.

First, he recognizes that he is a prisoner because he serves the Lord. This can be taken in two ways. Paul was writing this letter whilst he was under house arrest. He was physically imprisoned because he had refused to deny Christ and cease preaching the gospel. However, Paul also sees another kind of captivity. He is a captive of the Lord Jesus Christ. That is since the moment of his conversion he has belonged totally to Jesus and been committed to serving him and him alone. Such a willingness to be a servant of the Lord prevents us from becoming arrogant and self-important. We are constantly brought back to our total dependence upon him.

Gifts from the victory procession

The second reason for continuing humility comes in Paul's picture of the victory procession. As a Roman citizen, Paul would have seen many military processions headed by victorious commanders. It was the custom that at the end of the procession would come all the captives and spoils of war. As the procession came to its climax these would be given as gifts from the commander to his favourites.

Paul sees the return of Jesus to heaven as a great triumphant procession and as the victorious commander the Lord gives gifts to his people. Such a picture is a constant reminder that we have not created or invented the gifts ourselves but they have been given to us by the Lord for use in his service. This must constantly remind us of our need for humility as we use them.

Stable and mature

Paul is eager that the Ephesians, like the Corinthians, should understand the true nature of the gifts of the Spirit and also their true purpose. At the beginning of the passage he stresses the need for unity in the Spirit so that the Church can reflect the unity of God. However he recognizes that there is a great diversity, and the unity of the Spirit must be a continuing process. In Ephesians 4:13 he says, 'We shall all come together to that oneness in our faith.' The gifts are given that the Church might discover a unity which is both stable and mature.

Paul recognized that young Christians and young churches could easily be diverted from the truth and was constantly alert to this danger. His whole ministry was concerned with bringing the Church to a stability in Jesus Christ. This must be our concern today. All too often we see Christians and congregations being led by the latest fad and whim and so being diverted from the truth. As the gifts of the Spirit are exercised and the various ministries mentioned in verses 11–12 are present in a congregation, so the danger is averted because individuals and congregations are growing up into mature adult discipleship.

The fulness of Christ

It is always important to have a goal or aim. It is crucial to decide what the aim or goal of Church life is and what the ultimate purpose of the gifts of the Holy Spirit is. The answer is given loud and clear in this passage. The gifts are given so that the Church might reach the stature and maturity of Jesus himself. The very fulness of Christ will then reside in his Church. Moreover, as the gifts are exercised and the body grows, so there will be a deepening love, which is the sign of God's presence amongst his people.

Pause for thought

Paul saw himself as a prisoner for the Lord's sake. Are you willing to see your life in the same way? Record your feelings in your diary.

Pause for reflection

As a Church, are we willing to see the great diversity of gifts, and are you willing to offer your gift for the benefit of the whole? In what ways can you help others grow into maturity and stability?

Pause for prayer

Lord, so fill me with your Holy Spirit
that I might be the person you want me to be,
and do what you want me to do
within your body, the Church.
Amen.

Day 6

The Spirit in the life of a young church: Philippi

Philippians 2:1–11

> *The attitude you should have is the one that Christ Jesus had: He always had the nature of God, but he did not think that by force he should try to remain equal with God. Instead of this, of his own free will he gave up all he had, and took the nature of a servant.* (vv. 5–7)

In our last two studies this week we'll look at two examples of young churches in the New Testament. The churches in Philippi and Colossae were both encouragements to Paul although, as with all the churches, he is concerned about the threat of false teaching and writes to encourage them to remain firm and faithful.

Both churches would have been quite small numerically, set in an environment which was often hostile to the gospel. Both would have been seeking to work out the Christian faith and their discipleship in the context of a non-Christian society. The principles and issues which faced them were not so different from those that face the Church today, and that is why we can so readily learn from them.

A church growing in grace

In the opening verse of the letter, Paul rejoices that the Philippian church has been demonstrating signs of God's grace at work within them. They have shown an eagerness to share in the work of the gospel by sending Paul a gift of money and have continued to grow in the love of God. Paul recognizes that this is all the work of God's grace and prays that it will continue and bring the Philippians to full maturity.

The life of fellowship

At the opening of chapter 2, Paul writes that this life of grace and growing maturity is the work of Christ and the ministry of the Holy Spirit in the church: 'They have fellowship with the Spirit.' The Good News Bible footnote suggests this can also read, 'The Spirit has brought you into fellowship with one another.' The life which the Philippian church experienced was not of its own making but rather a gift of the Holy Spirit as he moved amongst them. Something of the life and quality of heaven was present in that little congregation. This depth and reality of fellowship expressed itself in very practical ways. The Holy Spirit gave them a kindness and compassion for one another. There may well have been vibrant worship in the church at Philippi and probably all the gifts and ministries of the Spirit were being exercised. But the thing which struck Paul most forcibly was the Philippians' willingness to be open and accepting one of another. This is an authentic mark of the Holy Spirit at work in a congregation and we need to pray for it earnestly for our own churches.

Paul, rejoicing at what the Spirit is doing in the life of the Philippians, encouraged them to move even further in the life of the Spirit. It is striking that the qualities he looked for were supremely practical—even mundane. Yet these are just the qualities and attitudes the Holy Spirit wants to produce in our churches. There must be a unity in our thinking and loving; the church which is threatened by selfish ambition will soon be divided and spoilt. Within the fellowship given by the Holy Spirit, openness and acceptance of each other should show themselves in humility and a willingness to build the self-esteem of another. These things may seem rather tame in comparison to the 'high profile' gifts, but they are absolutely vital if Christians are to demonstrate anything of the kingdom of heaven within the life of the Church.

The mind of Christ

As always, Paul brought his readers back to the model and example of Jesus himself. It is the Holy Spirit who makes the new quality of life possible, but it is in Jesus that we find the full demonstration of that life. Paul encouraged his readers to allow the Spirit to give them the mind of Jesus himself. Jesus, who did not stand on his rights and privileges, but rather became a servant and was willing to be humble and obedient and in the end give his life on the cross. Such a way and such an attitude are not the natural human pattern. It is impossible for us to create these attributes ourselves. Only if we know the filling of the Holy Spirit can our minds be renewed with the mind of Jesus.

Paul concludes this great passage with the reminder that Jesus is Lord and one day *all* will openly proclaim the acknowledgment of this Lordship. We are aware that such a recognition is not widespread today. It is only by the Spirit's power that Jesus can be recognized as Lord and only by the Spirit's power that we can proclaim that Lordship.

With the Philippian church, we need to know the power of the Holy Spirit to give us true fellowship with Christ and one another. Like the Philippian church we need to allow the Holy Spirit to fill our minds, that they might be constantly renewed, and our eyes and lips opened to recognize and proclaim that Jesus Christ is Lord.

Pause for thought

Are you growing in your discipleship and becoming more Christ-like? This is an important and fundamental question. Take time to pray before responding and recording your response in your diary.

Pause for reflection

God's power will lead you into a deeper understanding of his will. In what ways do you know your life so empowered by his Holy Spirit that you are growing in openness, acceptance and tolerance?

Pause for prayer

Lord, so fill me with your Holy Spirit
that I might, know your way more clearly,
walk with Jesus more closely,
and so become more like him in my attitude toward others.
Amen.

The Spirit in the life of a young church: Colossae

Colossians 1:1–14

For this reason we have always prayed for you, ever since we heard about you. We ask God to fill you with the knowledge of his will, with all the wisdom and understanding that his Spirit gives. Then you will be able to live as the Lord wants and will always do what pleases him. Your lives will produce all kinds of good deeds, and you will grow in your knowledge of God. (vv. 9–10)

Yesterday we looked at the church at Philippi and saw that many of the issues which faced it are the same issues that face us today. The spotlight now turns on the church at Colossae.

A dangerous setting

This young church had not been founded by Paul, but it was in a geographical area for which he had concern and so he sent them this letter. The opening verses show us that Paul was encouraged by what he had heard of the church's life. He gave thanks that their faith was growing, that they were sharing love for all God's people. However, he was concerned that the Colossians were in danger of falling into error. As with many of the other young churches, false teachers had either arrived or sprung up within the congregation. These false teachers were suggesting that it was necessary to worship spiritual beings other than Jesus and to submit to certain religious rights such as circumcision.

Paul was fearful that this young church would turn away from the truth. He encouraged the Christians in Colossae to hold on to the truth of Jesus and to recognize that he alone can bring forgiveness, and that only through his cross would creation be renewed. Paul prayed fervently for the Colossians and it is this prayer that is the subject of our study today.

The Spirit, wisdom and understanding

Spiritual issues can only be discerned and resolved by the power of the Holy Spirit. The threat of heresy facing the Colossians could only be overcome if they were open to God's Spirit. As with much false teaching over the centuries, and even in our own day, it is often so near the truth that it is hard to recognize the danger when it first occurs. It is only as our minds are filled with God's Spirit that the warning lights will flash and we will begin to recognize what is false and what is true.

We need to be constantly on the alert and recognize the issues as they arise. Some of the contemporary issues which face us include our understanding of the uniqueness of Christ and how we respond to those who want to put him alongside other gods. The Church is facing all the questions raised by 'New Age' teaching and the principles which lie behind it. We need to ask ourselves whether the outward rituals and forms which often become so important in Church life are really essential to the gospel of Jesus Christ. We need to ask whether things done in the name of Jesus and his Holy Spirit are indeed authentic.

Paul's prayer is as necessary for the Church today as it was for the church at Colossae. God's Holy Spirit brings with it wisdom, understanding and wise counsel. It is God's Holy Spirit who will enable the Church and individual Christians to set the issues against God's word and to see the truth.

A life of good fruit

There, is of course, no point in being theologically correct if that correctness does not display itself in a new quality of life. So often theology can become divorced from everyday living. Paul makes it quite clear that Christians who discern the truth through the Holy Spirit will be given power to live in a way that pleases God. Holding to the truth has a practical outworking and, as the Holy Spirit enables us to live life for the Lord, so we discover more about him. It is on the anvil of our everyday Christian experience that we discover more of God's grace and wisdom.

Strong to endure

From time to time we all wonder if we have the strength to go on. Sometimes life can seem very hard and discipleship becomes difficult and testing. At these points it is easy to draw back or to believe that God has abandoned us. Paul is both realistic and robust in his prayer. He knows that discipleship can be very tough and so he prays that his readers may know all the strength of God's glorious power so that they can endure everything—from the threat of physical persecution to the very real knocks and setbacks that come to all of us. Paul shows us that we should not simply press on with gritted teeth and grim determination. In the midst of hardship we can discover joy and the promise of heaven, if we ask the Holy Spirit to help us.

Looking forward

The Holy Spirit empowers us to live out our calling in this present age, and also gives us a foretaste of heaven. Paul emphasizes that our ultimate goal is heaven itself. It is to be this joy and certainty that encourages us to press on, no matter what the setbacks and disappointments. This is, of course, exactly the same emphasis as Jesus taught—our hearts must be set not on things on earth, but on heaven.

Sadly, for many Christians, heaven is such a remote possibility that it gives little encouragement for present discipleship. But if we truly ask the Holy Spirit to fill our hearts and minds we will have a foretaste of heaven, long for its fulness and find ourselves equipped to live the life to which God has called us.

Pause for thought

Reflect on this week of study on the Holy Spirit in the life of the Church. Are you willing to allow the Holy Spirit to disturb you so that you will seek more of God's power in your life? Reflect and then complete your diary. If you feel you need more of the Lord's power write your own prayer.

Pause for reflection

God longs to give his great gifts to individual disciples and to his

Church. In what ways are you open and willing to receive them? In what ways do you have a daily relationship with God and know the filling of his Holy Spirit?

Pause for prayer

If you feel that you would like to know the power of the Spirit quietly pray these words:

Spirit of the living God fall afresh on me,
Spirit of the living God fall afresh on me.
Break me, melt me, mould me, fill me,
Spirit of the living God fall afresh on me.
Daniel Iverson © Moody Bible Institute 1935, 1963

Lord, forgive all that's wrong in my life,
all that has displeased you.
I come now with my emptiness and hunger;
please fill me with your Holy Spirit.
Amen.

Having prayed that prayer, take time to be still and to be quiet to allow God's Spirit to move in you and fill you afresh. It might be helpful to talk to a trusted Christian friend or your minister about the step which you have taken.

Material for group study

For sharing

As individuals within the group, note down:

◇ the things that have been new to you and enlightened you

◇ the questions that have been raised.

Divide the group into pairs and give time for each pair to share their answers. Come together as a whole group for discussion and sharing.

For learning

Recapping on last week, take a drawing of a tree, place nine paper cut-outs of fruit with the qualities of the fruit of the Spirit listed on them. Share together the ways in which the Holy Spirit longs to transform our lives, not just as individuals, but also as part of the Church.

For discussion and application

List the gifts of the Spirit and put them alongside the diagram of the tree and fruit. What might the Lord be saying to the group about its own life? Or about the congregation of which it is part? Are there ways in which he wants to move us on in our discipleship, as individuals or as a congregation? How could this be allowed and encouraged to happen?

Are there areas of Church life which need to be touched by the Holy Spirit? Is your church willing to use the Spirit's gifts?

For prayer

In silence, wait upon the Lord. After a time of silence, either in open prayer or with prayer by the leader, ask God to fill you afresh with his Holy Spirit.

WEEK 6

THE HOLY SPIRIT IN MISSION

Archbishop William Temple said that the Church must exist for the sake of its non-members. The observation has also been made that the Church exists by mission as a fire exists by burning. In the New Testament we discover a Christian community where both those statements were true. There was a concern and care for the membership. The Church sought to build itself up in love, and there was a constant willingness to obey God's Holy Spirit and to move out into the world to proclaim the kingdom.

Zeal for mission is still to be found in many parts of the world today but, sadly, all too frequently in the West the Church has lost its cutting edge and has become inward looking. Some make the excuse that mission close to home is difficult, because of the secular nature of society; it has become hard to sing the Lord's song in a strange land. This statement is true to some extent, but the early Church was also working in a very hostile setting, as are many of our Christian brethren today. How can the fire of mission be rekindled in our churches?

God's agenda and the Spirit's work

In the last few years, the decade of evangelism has at least put mission back on the agenda. Within the Church of England financial crisis is causing some hard questions to be asked, though often for the wrong reasons. We may rejoice that mission is again under consideration, but for God, mission is not *on* the agenda—it *is* the agenda!

The Old Testament is the record of God's searching for lost men and women and his desire to build a community that would share in that task. This concern is continued in the New Testament. Jesus was constantly working amongst the lost and those whom the world had rejected. He came 'not to call the righteous, but sinners, to repent'. The Acts of the Apostles and the letters of the New Testament sound to the same tune. Issues of Church organization and questions of doctrine were important, but only as they vitally affected the work of mission. On the day of Pentecost, the fire of God fell upon the Church, equipping it to share the missionary heart of its Lord.

Cooperation and openness

God's heart beats for the lost, and the Church is called to share that heartbeat. Our studies this week, will show how the early Church allowed the Holy Spirit to fill it with the love of God for a lost and fallen world. There was a constant openness to the prompting of the Holy Spirit. Christians were prepared to change direction, cross frontiers and barriers, risk danger and even death, to proclaim the good news of Jesus. They simply wanted to discover where God was working, so that they could go and cooperate with his Spirit. The Church today needs to rediscover that openness and willingness to live a vibrant discipleship.

Mission and evangelism

Over the years there has been a very real confusion between these two words. Mission is the whole of God's work to the whole of his world, and explains why Christians find themselves involved in the world's needs and suffering in many different ways. Evangelism is the task of calling people to respond to God's love and the good news of Jesus Christ, in repentance and trust. As people experience something of God's love and work in their lives, so they need to respond to it in a deep personal way and know the promise of the Lord's forgiveness and the gift of his Holy Spirit.

Day 1

The Spirit and the mission at the heart of God

Luke 4:16–30

> *'He has sent me to proclaim liberty to the captives and recovery of sight to the blind; to set free the oppressed and announce that the time has come when the Lord will save his people.' Jesus rolled up the scroll, gave it back to the attendant, and sat down. All the people in the synagogue had their eyes fixed on him, as he said to them, 'This passage of scripture has come true today, as you heard it being read.'* **(vv. 18–21)**

A good pop song will have a catchy tune which will be repeated throughout, and will enable the listener to be at one with the message. So it is with the theme of mission. Throughout the Bible the song of mission is sung. There may be many different settings and aspects but always the reader is brought back to the one central theme. God is committed to his mission of restoring a broken creation and mending relationships with men and women. Jesus began his public ministry knowing that he was the key to God's strategic mission plan and that the power of the Holy Spirit was upon him enabling him to fulfil his calling.

The message of Jubilee

The passage which Jesus read from Isaiah spoke of the Jewish longing for 'Jubilee'. Jubilee was a promise deep in the roots of the Old Testament. The intention was that every fifty years land had to be returned to its original owner if it had been sold, and all those who were in debt or enslaved should be released. It would be a year of amnesty for prisoners and captives and a new start would be declared for every individual. Jubilee was linked with messianic expectation. The Messiah would usher in the true age of Jubilee when God would reclaim his people and release the enslaved.

Jesus saw his mission in terms of Jubilee. The captive would be set free, the prisoner released and the limiting effects of the fallen creation would be reversed—the deaf would hear and the blind would see. Above all, those who knew they were poor and in need of God's salvation and blessing would discover it. This had always been the desire of God the Father. It was to be fulfilled by the Son and empowered by the Holy Spirit.

The time has come

The really startling words for the congregation gathered in that little synagogue came at the end of the sermon: 'This passage of scripture has come true today, as you heard it being read.' Jesus claimed that the kingdom foretold and longed for in the Old Testament was being fulfilled in him. The mission of God, first recorded in Genesis as God sought for Adam and Eve in the Garden of Eden, was about to reach its climax in Jesus. The rest of Jesus' ministry was the demonstration of the truth of his claim; through his miracles the blind *did* see, the deaf *did* hear and the poor *did* receive the good news of God's forgiveness and salvation.

This work which Jesus began during his earthly ministry continues through his Church. The Holy Spirit which empowered Jesus now empowers the Church to proclaim the same message of Jubilee, and to continue to make God's missionary and searching heart known in the all world.

Pause for thought

In your diary note down the key things that speak to you in Jesus' message of Jubilee and your reactions to them.

Pause for reflection

Does the Church today sing the message of Jubilee? How could it 'sing the Lord's song' more effectively?

Pause for prayer

We have a gospel to proclaim
good news to men in all the earth.

Lord teach me and anoint me
to share in this work
of proclaiming your love and purpose.
Amen.

Day 2

The Holy Spirit: the author of mission

Matthew 28:16–20

'Go, then, to all peoples everywhere and make them my disciples: baptize them in the name of the Father, the Son, and the Holy Spirit, and teach them to obey everything I have commanded you. And I will be with you always, to the end of the age.' **(vv. 19–20)**

On the day of his ascension, Jesus met with his disciples and gave them his final command, in what has been termed 'the great commission'. His words set the agenda for his Church for the rest of human history. The missionary concern at the heart of God is to become the agenda for the Christian Church. The Lord Jesus Christ gave the Church the authority to share in the task of making disciples. His Church is the instrument whereby everyone is to be told of God's love and called to respond to it.

Note that the command is to 'make disciples', not to 'make Christians' or 'Church members'. The word 'disciple' implies someone who has become a fully rounded and devoted follower of Jesus Christ; a person ready to listen to his word and to allow his or her life to be marked by his example. The aim of God's mission is to bring men and women into special relationship with him and to enable their lives to reflect the likeness of Jesus Christ.

For this to happen the three persons of the Trinity need to be present in mission and ministry. New disciples need to be baptized into:

◇ the Father who wills their new life.

◇ the Son who earns for them the right to new life.

◇ the Holy Spirit who enables them to receive and then to grow in new life.

For all the world

Jesus' great commission stresses the universal nature of God's mission. We are called to travel into every part of the world to win disciples for Jesus. The good news of Jesus is truly for all the world, not simply in terms of geography, but also for all times and generations. The Lord of the great commission is the one who will be with his followers 'until the end of the age'. This means until the present course of history comes to its end with the return of Jesus and the advent of the new heaven and the new earth. Those who recognize the importance of God's mission today to this generation are direct descendants of the disciples who received the great commission on a hill in Galilee.

Power from on high

How is it possible to take God's mission is to every generation and every place? The disciples who first heard Jesus' commission found that at first it made little difference to their frightened and weak lives. They may have been filled with joy, but they knew little of boldness. How were their lives changed so that they became agents for God's mission?

It was as the power of the Holy Spirit fell upon them that the disciples became gripped by God's desire to reach out into his world. They did not 'proclaim the great things of God' on the day of Pentecost, because they thought they *ought* to or because they considered it a good idea, but because the Holy Spirit left them no choice. His power burned within them and inevitably they were seized with the desire to share in God's work of reaching those who did not know his love, to offer them the gift of his grace and the promise of his Holy Spirit.

The Holy Spirit was the initiator of the work of mission in the early Church. God's call to his people, which had flowed from his heart from the beginning of time and found its focus in Jesus, was entering a new dimension as men and women found themselves caught up with God's work in his world.

A missionary Spirit

The Acts of the Apostles is the record of God's Holy Spirit in the missionary activity of the early Church. No mission initiative is taken without his leading. No new area of work is opened up unless he first shows where Christians are meant to go. There is a sense of the Holy Spirit's dynamism in mission and the Church's anticipation and expectation to see him at work.

Further reading

Acts 1:6–11; 11:19–24

Pause for thought

Are you willing to allow God's Holy Spirit to use you in the work of mission? Write your response in your diary.

Pause for reflection

The gospel of Jesus is for every generation and every nation. What are the limits we place upon the gospel? Do we know the 'power from on high' compelling us to speak out the good news of Jesus?

Pause for prayer

O Breath of life come sweeping through us
Revive thy church with life and power.
O Breath of life come cleanse renew us
And fit thy church to meet this hour.

Elizabeth Porter Head

Day 3

The Spirit and crossing the boundaries

Acts 11:1–18

The apostles and the other believers throughout Judea heard that the Gentiles also had received the word of God. When Peter went to Jerusalem, those who were in favour of circumcising Gentiles criticized him, saying, 'You were a guest in the home of uncircumcised Gentiles, and you even ate with them!' So Peter gave them a complete account of what had happened from the very beginning. **(vv. 1–4)**

To understand the full content of Peter's report to the church at Jerusalem you will need to read the whole of Acts 10.

God intends his message of love to be proclaimed universally across the nations and down the ages. This has been a great challenge to the Church in every generation and is no less a challenge to the Church in our own day. Those of us who call ourselves Christian disciples need to heed the challenge, discover how we can meet it and so continue to be used in God's mission.

A world of frontiers

The world in which we live is made up of frontiers and barriers. There are national frontiers which mark out countries and which require passports and visas if we are to cross them. As well as these well-defined frontiers there are a host of others barriers in our world. There are frontiers and barriers between races and religions. Nations discover there are barriers and frontiers within their national life—barriers of class, of status, of social or ethnic background.

As well as the enormous barriers and frontiers there are also local and personal divisions. The local church can find itself divided over many different issues and it can seem impossible to reach out over the frontiers. Individuals and families can raise similar impenetrable barriers and many feel isolated and without hope.

The world in which the early Church was born was one of great division and barriers. In one sense the Roman Empire had united the known world, but within that great empire there were splinter groups where people hid behind the barriers to find a personal and national sense of stability, identity and security.

The first Christian disciples were born into a Jewish setting and as such were surrounded by many different frontiers. As Jews they would have kept themselves away from the Samaritan and Gentile worlds and there would have been little expectation that the missionary Spirit of God would call them to scale the walls of division and cross into new territories—but this is precisely what the Holy Spirit demanded!

Across the barriers

The disciples had witnessed the ministry of Jesus and seen how he had crossed many of the cultural, social, religious, political and national divides. He had spoken to outcasts—those who were ritually unclean—to sinners and to foreigners. Throughout his ministry he demonstrated that the mission of God was to transcend every human division. Although they had seen this mission strategy modelled in the life of Jesus, the early Church were taken by surprise when they found themselves called to exactly the same pattern.

When Peter went onto the roof to pray (Acts 10:9) he had no expectation that God was about to turn all his preconceptions upside down. With the arrival of the visitors from Cornelius, Peter found himself thrown into the Gentile world. He was even more amazed when the Holy Spirit fell upon Cornelius and his household whilst he was still speaking!

Peter wasn't the only one to experience this crossing of the great divide. Philip found himself on a mission to Samaria and then in the desert speaking to an Ethiopian eunuch and leading him to faith; Paul and Barnabas were commissioned by the Church under the authority of the Holy Spirit to become missionaries to the Gentiles—Paul eventually preaching in Rome itself.

Waiting for the Spirit

In all these instances it was the Holy Spirit who led the early Church to climb over human divisions and proclaim the kingdom on the other side of the frontier. If the Church today is to be empowered in the same way it is crucial that it should be willing to wait upon the Lord and expect the Spirit to lead it forward. So much of our Church decision-making has little to do with God or his Spirit and prayer is often far from the heart of the Church. As a consequence the barriers stay firmly in place and the proclamation of the kingdom is entrenched in the sphere of the Church rather than going beyond its frontiers into God's world.

It was as the early Church prayed, fasted and waited upon God that he was able to lead it forward. We need to learn the lesson of waiting for the Holy Spirit and then obeying his voice if we want to be a true instrument of mission in God's hands.

Change and challenge

One of the reasons that we may find it easier to stay behind the barriers is because to move across the frontiers brings change and challenge. Peter rejoiced that Cornelius and his household experienced God's grace in the gift of the Spirit. However, Peter had to face the leaders of the Jerusalem church who were at first hostile to what had happened. All of us find change difficult to handle and cope with. For many, living in a world of bewildering change, Church life becomes a bastion of stability. This is not God's way or desire. He is constantly wanting to move us on into new areas in the power of his Holy Spirit. We need to learn a willing obedience and to realize that our true stability is in him alone and not in the structure of Church life, which all too frequently becomes a barrier to God's mission in his world.

Pause for thought

In your diary write down the barriers and frontiers in your own life. Are you willing to cross them in the power of the Holy Spirit?

Pause for reflection

Do you find change difficult—if so why? How can the Holy Spirit help you to be prepared to change and move on? In your diary did you discover frontiers you are unwilling to cross? Did this become a matter for urgent prayer? Does your church show a willingness to reach out across the barriers?

Pause for prayer

Lord, thank you that in your love
you crossed the greatest barrier,
the barrier of my sin,
and brought me back to yourself.
Give me the courage,
by the power of your Holy Spirit,
to cross every barrier I know
to bring your love to others.
Amen.

Day 4

The Holy Spirit in the world

John 16:7–15

'I am telling you the truth: it is better for you that I go away, because if I do not go, the Helper will not come to you. But if I do go away, then I will send him to you. And when he comes, he will prove to the people of the world that they are wrong about sin and about what is right and about God's judgement.' (vv. 7–8)

We often think that the Holy Spirit is the possession of the Church alone. But the New Testament makes it clear that, whereas the Church is indeed the recipient of the Holy Spirit, God's Spirit is always at work in his world, beyond the confines of the Church. It is important to understand the Holy Spirit's work within the world so that we may cooperate with him more fully and more effectively.
In today's key verses we see that the Holy Spirit is given to the Church as a 'Helper' or 'Comforter', but is given to the world as a 'Prosecutor'. Jesus taught that the Holy Spirit has to be at work in an individual's life if that person is to come to faith in him. This quickening power of the Holy Spirit is absolutely vital. The Holy Spirit is the one who brings life and understanding, and also reveals that the people of the world are under God's condemnation. These are strong words and we need to examine their truth.

The witness of Jesus and the disciples

Jesus pointed both to the reality of the one who had sent him and the power of the kingdom he had come to bring. There were many—including the religious leaders—who saw the evidence and yet still opposed Jesus' ministry. This opposition went so far as to claim that Jesus was not empowered by the Holy Spirit, but he performed his miracles through the authority of Satan. This frightening reversal of the truth left Jesus to conclude that people had missed God's moment when it came, and also that they were in danger of blasphemy against the Holy Spirit. Jesus promised that when the

'Helper' came to the disciples they would find themselves speaking about Jesus, sharing in his work and demonstrating the power of the kingdom. People would speak against them as they had Jesus, but nevertheless the disciples' example would stand as a witness to the truth. The work of the Holy Spirit in their lives would vindicate the claims Jesus had made. After Pentecost, the lives of Spirit-filled disciples would be like a witness for the prosecution against those in the world who denied the truth of Jesus. Jesus explained the threefold nature of this to them.

Sin

First, Jesus explained that the people of the world held the wrong view about sin. Sin is not just acts of wrong which are committed by the individual, but is ultimately the rejection of the centrality of Jesus. In the final analysis God's dealing with sin will be based upon the individual's attitude and response to Jesus. Belief (or trust, as it means in John's Gospel) brings with it the promise of forgiveness and new life—unbelief carries with it the fact of God's condemnation.

Righteousness

Secondly, Jesus demonstrated that he alone is able to open the 'kingdom of heaven' to all believers. Those who condemned Jesus thought he was unrighteous and his condemnation and punishment a just reward. Such an attitude marked those who signed the actual death warrant and crucified him. It also marks those who down the centuries have failed to recognize the significance and importance of his death and resurrection. Through his own righteousness, Jesus alone is able to put us right with God and open the kingdom of heaven to all believers.

Judgment

Lastly, Jesus showed that through his death and resurrection he defeated the power of Satan once and for all. To fail to recognize that defeat is to fail to recognize the true nature and purpose of Jesus. Those who crucified him failed to recognize that a great cosmic struggle between the forces of darkness and the power of light was taking place on the cross. Through the cross, the 'ruler of this world'—Satan—has already been judged.

These three things are central to God's missionary desire. If people do not understand what sin is, nor accept that only through the cross of Christ can they be put right with God, then there can be no real discipleship. The Holy Spirit enables the Christian disciple to join with his own witness to the truth of Jesus and so bring the prosecution of the world to a successful conclusion. It is only as people begin to recognize their guilt that they can respond to God in a new way. This is the other side of the Holy Spirit's work, which will be the study for tomorrow.

Pause for thought

In your diary write down how you feel about 'sin', 'righteousness' and 'judgment'.

Pause for reflection

Why are men and women lost without Jesus? How does the witness of the Holy Spirit show the guilt of the world? How can we cooperate with the Holy Spirit as he works in God's world?

Pause for prayer

Lord, teach me to see the world as you see it
and then by the power of your Holy Spirit
give me your heart of love for your world.
Amen.

Day 5

The Holy Spirit: mind and word

2 Corinthians 4:1–7

In the full light of truth we live in God's sight and try to commend ourselves to everyone's good conscience. For if the gospel we preach is hidden, it is hidden only from those who are being lost. They do not believe, because their minds have been kept in the dark by the evil god of this world. He keeps them from seeing the light shining on them, the light that comes from the Good News about the glory of Christ, who is the exact likeness of God... Yet we who have this spiritual treasure are like common clay pots, in order to show that the supreme power belongs to God, not to us. **(vv. 2–4, 7)**

The Holy Spirit longs to bring people to new life. In this task he is continuing the missionary work of God in reaching out to touch lives with grace and truth.

The great battle

There is often little sense in the contemporary Church in the West of the great battle which continues to be waged between the forces of light and darkness—between Satan and the living God. Many would dismiss this kind of teaching as totally out of place in today's world.

Yet Jesus saw himself involved in a constant battle against Satan. His public ministry was preceded by the temptations which were a key stage in the formation of his thinking and understanding. He rejoiced when the disciples returned triumphant from a period of mission, saying that he had seen Satan fall like lightning—it was as though he believed the hold of Satan upon the world was beginning to slip. This hold received its final blow on the cross, where he defeated the power of sin in the life of the individual, and destroyed the strangle hold of Satan upon creation.

Although the power of Satan was defeated upon the cross, there is a sense in which that power will not finally be utterly destroyed until the return of Christ. So it is that Paul can speak about Christians not 'wrestling with flesh and blood but against principalities and powers'. This great battle is the continuing context for mission and the context in which the Holy Spirit works.

The great light

The victims of the great battle are those who Satan keeps in darkness, preventing them from seeing the light. However the light has come and continues to shine in and through the person of Jesus Christ. He is the light of the world and one in whom the light of God shines in all its fulness. It is this light and the good news which it brings which is the message of the Church. As the message is preached, so the Holy Spirit is at work, shining God's light into individual hearts, to bring us to 'the knowledge of God's glory shining in the face of Christ' (2 Corinthians 4:6).

In the context of the great battle, the Father, Son and Holy Spirit come together in the life of an individual to bring the reality of forgiveness and new life.

The great message

The light dawns as the Church faithfully preaches the message of Jesus Christ as Lord. Throughout the New Testament the preaching of the word is closely linked with the ministry and work of the Holy Spirit. On the day of Pentecost, Peter preached in the power of the Holy Spirit. Some of his hearers were 'deeply troubled' because the Spirit had brought God's word alive to them—and their hearts and minds alive to God's Word. It was this divine partnership which led to repentance and rebirth.

So it must be today. The Church needs to cooperate with the missionary God. We need to pray that those who preach will know the anointing of God's Holy Spirit. We also need to pray that unbelievers will know the illuminating influence of the Holy Spirit and so have their hearts and minds prepared to accept and receive the word.

The great service

In all our studies we have seen that the Spirit of God is an integral part of the power of the personal God, who comes to create the person and characteristics of Jesus himself in the Church and in the life of each believer. One of the greatest characteristics of Jesus is his willingness to serve.

Paul shows us that in order to cooperate with the Spirit of God in mission we must be willing to become like servants. Our lives must have an integrity and authenticity, and a willingness to be a servant of others for Jesus' sake. It is only as the Church becomes this community of service that the missionary Spirit of the missionary God can bring people to new life.

Further reading

Acts 2:37; 10:44

Pause for thought

Take a moment to meditate on the light of God which shines through Jesus. Write down in your diary the way his light illuminates your life and how you long for it to illuminate others.

Pause for reflection

What are the signs of the continuing struggle between the power of darkness and the power of light? Why does the word of God make a difference? How can we enable the Holy Spirit to help others to receive it? Are you willing to become a servant of the Lord and to cooperate with his Holy Spirit so that others may receive his light and life?

Pause for prayer

'Out of darkness the light shall shine' (2 Corinthians 4:6).

Lord shine in my heart
by the power of your Holy Spirit
and let me be your servant
to bring others to the same knowledge.
Amen.

Day 6

The Holy Spirit and signs and wonders

Luke 10:1–12, 17–20

> *After this the Lord chose another 72 men and sent them out two by two, to go ahead of him to every town and place where he himself was about to go. He said to them, 'There is a large harvest, but few workers to gather it in. Pray to the owner of the harvest that he will send out workers to gather in his harvest... The 72 men came back in great joy. 'Lord,' they said, 'even the demons obeyed us when we gave them a command in your name!'* (vv. 1–2, 17)

The question of signs and wonders and unusual manifestations of the Holy Spirit is very much at the forefront of Christian thinking and debate at the present moment. Such signs and wonders might include healing and exorcism as well as seemingly personal experiences of the Holy Spirit such as speaking in tongues, acting as though drunk, feelings of exhilaration and even being 'knocked over' by the power of the Spirit. Some feel that signs and wonders are so integral to the mission of God that they must be actively sought and developed. Others believe that whilst the Lord may do remarkable things, signs and wonders as such should not be actively encouraged. Others feel that signs and wonders died out with the apostles and they would regard any such manifestations today with deep distrust. Are there any insights and principles from the New Testament to help us through this maze?

Signs of the kingdom

Jesus preached the kingdom not only with words but also with signs and deeds. He looked for the blind to see and the deaf to hear and for the captive to be set free. He demonstrated the kingdom's power by deed and action—the disabled were made whole, the hungry were fed, the dead were raised and the poor received the good news of the kingdom.

The signs of the kingdom were evident in the mission of the seventy-two. The extended band of followers was sent out to proclaim the kingdom and told that part of that proclamation was to heal the sick. As the mission drew to a close the disciples returned rejoicing in all that they had seen and experienced. They were amazed at the authority of Jesus' name over evil.

Jesus' response to this celebration was to rejoice that Satan's grip on the world was being broken. The spiritual battle fought in the heavenly realm as well as on earth began to turn in favour of the power of the living God with Satan being expelled from heaven. However, Jesus gives us all a word of warning. The disciples were to rejoice, not because the demons obeyed, but because their names were written in heaven.

We should expect that wherever the kingdom is proclaimed we will see signs of that kingdom breaking in. The sign though is not the prime factor. The important issue is that the person has been put right with God and has the certainty of heaven.

Making people whole

The kingdom comes in the name of the Lord Jesus in order that people might be made whole. The fundamental 'wholeness' which they need is the forgiveness of sin and the assurance that their guilt has been removed and is no longer a barrier between them and heaven. Once Satan's grasp on the life of an individual has been broken then the power of God's kingdom can break in, in all its fulness.

Of course, even those who were healed by Jesus subsequently died. Any experience of healing and wholeness here on earth is only a foretaste of what will be totally ours in heaven. We pray 'may your kingdom come on earth as it is in heaven'. At the present time we see signs of that kingdom which will be made complete when Christ returns. The breaking in of the kingdom is about restoring people to the wholeness God intends for them: first, spiritual wholeness by means of his forgiveness; then an expectation that as the kingdom takes root in the power of the Holy Spirit, there will be expressions of his healing and transformation.

Seek first the kingdom

As we see God's kingdom coming and expect signs of the kingdom it is crucial that our basic motivation is to seek his will above everything else. It is so easy to seek a particular experience or long for a particular manifestation of God's Spirit. It may well be that he wants to deal in that way in our lives, but equally he may have a totally different route for our particular discipleship.

We must not deny the power of the Holy Spirit, nor limit him because of our prejudice and fear. Rather we are to seek God's will in all things and be prepared to accept, enjoy and use aright any blessings which he, in his grace, showers upon us.

Further reading

Luke 4:16–19; 7:18–23; Acts 2:43; 4:30; 5:12

Pause for thought

Do you find the thought of God acting in signs and wonders disturbing or encouraging? Write down your reactions in your diary.

Pause for reflection

In what ways might the Lord want to act today to display the power of his kingdom? What are the signs and wonders we should expect to see in our churches today? Are we concerned for people to become 'whole'?

Pause for prayer

Lord Jesus, help me to be
a willing instrument in your hands,
that your kingdom might come
on earth as it is in heaven.
Lord, may your kingdom come
in the way that you desire.
Amen.

Day 7

The Holy Spirit and witness

1 Corinthians 2:1–5

When I came to you, my brothers and sisters, to preach God's secret truth, I did not use big words and great learning. For while I was with you, I made up my mind to forget everything except Jesus Christ and especially his death on the cross. (vv. 1–2)

Many of us find speaking about our faith very hard, and yet Peter encourages us to be ready to give a reason for our Christian hope (1 Peter 3:15). It may be that we are not sure that we have that hope, and we need to seek God's Spirit to know the assurance of hope which he brings. It may be that we know the hope but cannot express it. It is important for Christians to study and to equip themselves. However, in the final analysis, if we have experienced the hope which God's Spirit gives, then however halting our words, our witness will be effective and used by God. Part of sharing in God's mission in his world is the willingness to speak about him. Today's study gives four areas for encouragement.

With knocking knees

In his first letter to the Corinthians, Paul recalls his initial visit to their city. Scholars have suggested that, as Paul's visit to Corinth followed his unhappy visit to Athens, he had lost some of his confidence and this explains his feelings of inadequacy and fear. Whatever the precise reason, it is an encouragement to know that even the great apostle Paul knew times of difficulty and lacked self-confidence. But for him his fear did not become an excuse for withdrawing from witnessing and preaching. Paul's fear threw him back to rely solely on God, where he discovered that God's power enabled him to overcome his personal inadequacies. Similarly, in our weakness and fear we need to turn back to total dependence upon God's Spirit, rather than allowing our witness to be stifled.

The Lord's power was with them

Like Paul, the early Church had a genuine excuse to keep quiet. Persecution had intensified following the death of Stephen and the comfort of the Church was shattered. Believers found themselves fleeing for their lives, but nevertheless continued to share the gospel. Indeed, far from being a hindrance to Church growth, the persecution became a catalyst for the word to spread. The gospel was preached to the Jews and Gentiles, and the Christians experienced the Lord's power with them. The Lord who empowered the witness of those early Christians longs to empower the witness of his people today.

Constrained by love

We can very easily feel pressurized into witnessing by Church leaders. This is unhelpful and potentially destructive because witnessing done out of a sense of duty immediately loses its authenticity and spontaneity. The early Christians did not feel under a duty or obligation to witness—it was a natural desire. They were 'ruled by the love of Christ, now that we recognize that one man died for everyone, which means that all share in his death' (2 Corinthians 5:14).

There will be no reality or power in our witness if it does not flow from a heart that is both full of love from God and full of love for God. Just as a couple in love radiate their affection for each other, so it must be in Christian witness. We are simply telling others of our relationship with Jesus. This gift of love which will not allow us to keep silent is the work of the Holy Spirit, for it is he who pours God's love into our hearts.

Pointing to the truth

In the end, our witness does not point to ourselves with all our failings and weaknesses, but to the Lord Jesus Christ. We are called to speak of the absolute truths of the gospel which are not dependent on who we are or how we feel. The good news we share is of Christ's death and resurrection, his ascension, the gift of his Holy Spirit and the promise of his coming again. It is through these great events that God has made it possible for humankind to be reconciled to himself. This is the heart of the gospel message and the Holy Spirit longs to empower us to proclaim it.

Further reading

Acts 11:19–21; 2 Corinthians 5:11–21; 1 Peter 3:15

Pause for thought

In your diary write down the things you enjoy about being a witness for the Lord Jesus and the things you find hard.

Pause for reflection

Despite our feelings of weakness and inadequacy, the Holy Spirit longs to use us to proclaim the gospel message. Where is it possible for you to be a witness? In what ways could you ask the Lord to open the doors of opportunity?

Pause for prayer

Lord, I often feel weak and ineffective
in my witness for you,
and yet I want to be able
to proclaim your good news faithfully and boldly.
Thank you that your Spirit is there to empower me.
Please teach me to be open to him day by day.
Amen.

Material for group study

For sharing

As individuals within the group, note down:

◇ the things that have been new to you and enlightened you

◇ the questions that have been raised.

Divide the group into pairs and give time for each pair to share their answers.

For learning

As a group take a large sheet of card. Write on it in single words or phrases the new things you have learnt about the Holy Spirit during this week.

On a second sheet of card, on which is either a picture or photograph of your church, write down the areas of mission in which the Holy Spirit needs to enrich or renew your congregation.

For discussion and application

Take the results from above and then in pairs discuss how you might implement the change in a loving and caring way.

Come together as a group and share your findings. Try and identify three or four main issues which you would like to take further.

For prayer

As this is the final week of the course you might like to share an informal eucharistic or *agape* meal. As well as the bread and the wine you could set out some items which depict the symbols of the Holy Spirit: water, oil, fire, light, a picture of a dove and so on. In a time of prayer, each of these symbols of the Holy Spirit could be used to give thanks for his ongoing ministry. Spend some time praying, either quietly or aloud, for his renewal and deepening within the life of the individual and the local church.

APPENDIX I: THE GIFTS OF THE SPIRIT

Below are listed some twenty gifts which the Holy Spirit gives to the Church. Obviously no individual Christian will possess all, and particular gifts may be given to individuals for a certain time and purpose. Further, the gifts listed in the New Testament are not necessarily an exhaustive catalogue of all the Holy Spirit is able to give. Often individual Christians will have more than one gift which complement each other and so bring a greater richness to the body of Christ.

Under the heading for each gift there is a brief description. The Bible references indicate where the gift is listed and, in most cases, there is a biblical example of how the gift was used.

Administration

The gift of administration is the God-given ability to organize and support the wider ministry of the Church through practical management which increases the effectiveness of the whole Church.

Reference: 1 Corinthians 12:28
Example: Acts 6:1–7

Apostleship

Some people believe that the term 'apostle' can only be applied to those who were witnesses to the resurrection. However, whilst that may be a particular and special use of the term, it does appear that the New Testament recognized those with a special gift of leadership which goes beyond the confines of the local congregation and is used to build and establish the Church.

Reference: 1 Corinthians 12:28–29; Ephesians 4:11–12
Example: Romans 16:7

Discernment

A gift which enables the Church member to differentiate between good and evil. This might be used in any situation where the truth of an issue is not clear, but it is particularly useful in recognizing whether spiritual gifts and insights are actually the work of the Holy Spirit.
Reference: 1 Corinthians 12:10
Example: Acts 5:3

Encouragement

The gift of encouragement is the God-given ability to affirm someone in their calling or activity and to literally give them courage to continue.
Reference: Romans 12:8
Example: Acts 15:32

Evangelism

The gift of evangelism enables people clearly to explain the work of Jesus Christ to non-believers, and then to help them respond personally to the Gospel.
Reference: Ephesians 4:11
Example: Acts 8:26–40

Faith

All are called to put their trust in Christ, but the gift of faith is the ability to trust God's promises and to act on them, even in the midst of difficulties. Those with the gift of faith are a particular blessing to the local church if it is facing a time of crisis, or believes God is calling it to a new piece of work or project, which in human terms seem impossible.
Reference: 1 Corinthians 12:9
Example: Hebrews 11
(a great catalogue of Old Testament saints who displayed faith)

Giving

The gift of giving releases those who receive it to give money and other resources with a great sense of liberality and rejoicing.

Reference: Romans 12:8

Example: Luke 21:1–4; 2 Corinthians 8:1–5

Healing

The God-given gift of healing enables people to experience the wholeness which God longs for them, whether of body, mind and spirit.

Reference: 1 Corinthians 12:9

Example: Acts 3:1–8

Helps

Closely linked to administration, this is the gift which offers ungrudging support in many practical ways, and so allows the body of Christ to grow more effectively.

Reference: 1 Corinthians 12:28; Romans 12:7

Example: Acts 6:1–7

Hospitality

A God-given willingness and ability to welcome others, especially strangers into the home. The gift of hospitality reflects the warmth and welcome we find in Jesus.

Reference: Romans 12:13; 1 Peter 4:9

Example: Hebrews 13:1–2

Intercession

All Christians are called to prayer, but it does seem that the Holy Spirit equips some with the ability to persist in prayer, and plead on behalf of the Church and the world.

Reference: Romans 8:26–27

Example: Acts 12:5

Interpretation
This gift allows the recipient to translate any message given in tongues during a church meeting. Through the exercising of this gift the message becomes of value and blessing to the whole church.
Reference: 1 Corinthians 12:10; 14:5

Knowledge
The gift to recognize and then communicate a 'heavenly' truth to the church. This knowledge is not a new additional revelation of God and must be in line with the touchstone of scripture.
Reference: 1 Corinthians 12:8

Leadership
The gift of leadership provides the Church with those who have gift of vision and insight, and enables others to attain their God-given calling.
Reference: Romans 12:8
Example: Acts 14:23

Mercy
An ability to care for people in a sensitive and appropriate manner.
Reference: Romans 12:8

Miracles
The God-given ability to call for exceptional and unexpected signs of God's power, which bring glory to God and blessing to the church or individual.
Reference: 1 Corinthians 12:28–29
Example: Acts 14:3

Prophecy
The God-given ability to speak God's word either in the church or to the individual. The prophet will speak with authority of God's Spirit, will be in accord with God's revelation of himself in scripture, and will seek to lead to correction, repentance or to build up the Church.
Reference: Romans 12:6; 1 Corinthians 12:10; Ephesians 4:11
Example: Acts 11:27–29; Acts 13:1–4

Shepherd/Pastor

As a shepherd cares for his flock and individual sheep, so the Spirit-gifted pastor seeks to protect and build the Christians committed to his/her care, both individually and as a community.

Reference: Ephesians 4:11; 1 Peter 5:1–4
Example: Acts 20:28–31

Teacher

Closely linked with pastor, the teacher, gifted by the Holy Spirit, is able to explain clearly the word of God and enable others to grasp it and so grow to maturity in their Christian faith and discipleship.

Reference: Romans 12:7; 1 Corinthians 12:28; Ephesians 4:11
Example: Acts 18:24–28

Tongues

The God-given gift to speak in an unknown language. This gift can be used in personal praise and prayer, and in public meetings of the church, when it should be interpreted.

Reference: 1 Corinthians 12:10
Example: Acts 2:1–13

Wisdom

Those gifted by the Holy Spirit to know God's word and apply it appropriately and wisely in given situations.

Reference: 1 Corinthians 12:8
Example: Acts 6:3, 10

APPENDIX II: THE TORONTO BLESSING

During the writing of this book, the phenomenon known as the 'Toronto Blessing' has touched many congregations and individuals both in this country and elsewhere in the world. Many claim that this movement is a new outpouring of God's Holy Spirit, and have been encouraged by the experience. Others have been sceptical and felt that the manifestations shown were little to do with God's Holy Spirit, and indeed were bizarre and unhelpful.

Whenever God's Spirit moves, or is claimed to be moving, there are always reactions for and against. Many of the physical expressions witnessed over the last few months have been experienced in previous periods of renewal and refreshing. On this occasion, as in the past there will be excuses and false claims.

It is always important to ask whether an apparent movement of the Spirit is of God. There are several criteria which can be applied:

◇ Is the movement in line with the teaching of scripture, and do the claims of those speaking under the influence of the Spirit centre on Jesus?

◇ Is the Church being enriched as a result of the movement? Is there an increasing desire for holiness in the life of the disciple, and a renewed zeal and power in the proclamation of the good news of Jesus Christ?

◇ Is each individual seeking the various manifestations for themselves or for the glorifying of the Lord Jesus Christ. Have the gifts become more important than the giver?

The authentic work of the Holy Spirit is to create holiness in the life and witness of the believer. Whenever we open ourselves to the power of God the Holy Spirit we need to remember that, like the wind, he will blow as he wills. He may come like a rushing mighty hurricane, or as a gentle evening breeze. It is not our place to criticize the way that God works in an individual's life, nor is it our place to demand a similar experience in our own life.